# THE GERMAN POPULAR PLAY
## *ATIS*
# AND THE VENETIAN OPERA

PLATE I

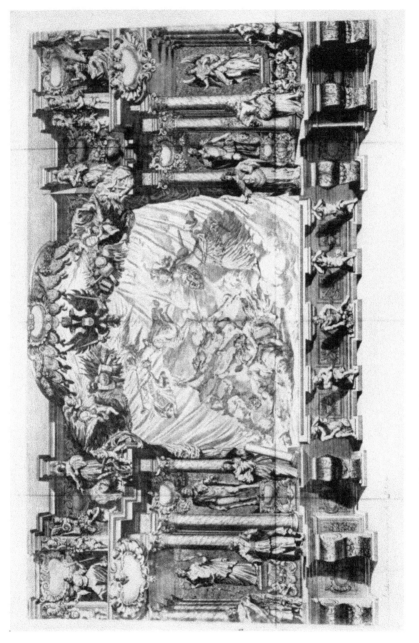

'Il Fuoco Eterno Custodito dalle Vestali.' Proscenium and Curtain

# THE
# GERMAN POPULAR PLAY
## *A T I S*
# AND THE VENETIAN OPERA

*A Study of the Conversion of Operas into Popular
Plays, 1675–1722, with special reference to the
play* Atis

BY

## MARY BEARE
*Fellow of Newnham College, Cambridge*

## CAMBRIDGE
AT THE UNIVERSITY PRESS
1938

# CAMBRIDGE
## UNIVERSITY PRESS

University Printing House, Cambridge CB2 8BS, United Kingdom

Published in the United States of America by Cambridge University Press, New York

Cambridge University Press is part of the University of Cambridge.

It furthers the University's mission by disseminating knowledge in the pursuit of
education, learning and research at the highest international levels of excellence.

www.cambridge.org
Information on this title: www.cambridge.org/9781107659025

© Cambridge University Press 1938

First published 1938
First paperback edition 2014

*A catalogue record for this publication is available from the British Library*

ISBN 978-1-107-65902-5 Paperback

# CONTENTS

*Preface*                                                    *page* ix

*Introduction*                                                     xi

*Chapter* I. A. Description of MS., authorship, date,
                  provenance                                       1
         B. Italian influence on the arts in Vienna               4

      II. Origin and structural elements of the
          Venetian Opera                                           8

     III. A. The "Mise-en-scène" of the Venetian
             Opera                                                14
          B. The Jesuit Drama and the Opera at
             Vienna                                               23

      IV. The Opera at Vienna and the Popular
          Theatre                                                 29

       V. 'Der Stumme Prinz Atis'; its relation to
          the Hamburg Opera and the Popular
          Theatre in Vienna                                       42

      VI. Analysis of the structural elements of 'Atis';
          comparison with the Italian original 'Creso'
          and with Bostel's 'Croesus'                             46

*Conclusion*                                                      66

*List of Libretti and "Haupt- und Staatsaktionen"*               73

*Bibliography*                                                    74

*Index*                                                           79

# ILLUSTRATIONS

PLATE

I. 'Il Fuoco Eterno Custodito dalle Vestali.'
Proscenium and Curtain        *frontispiece*
Photograph of engraving by Matthäus Küsel

II. 'La Gara.' Interior of the Theatre.
Tournament Scene       *facing page* 18
Photograph of engraving by Giovanni Burnacini

III. 'Il Pomo d'Oro.' Interior of the Theatre
Photograph of engraving by Franz Geffels

*between pages*

IV. 'Il Pomo d'Oro.' "Schaubinne des Öster-   20 *and* 21
reichischen Ehrn-Ruhms." Prologue
Photograph of engraving by Matthäus Küsel

V. 'La Monarchia Latina Trionfante.'
Prologue       *facing page* 22
Photograph of engraving by Matthäus Küsel

*All the illustrations are reproduced by courtesy of the National-Bibliothek in Vienna*

## PREFACE

If the pages that follow seem, as the sub-title indicates, to insist on the conversion of Italian operas into popular plays in the German language during the period under review, rather than on the play in question, it is for the simple reason that 'Atis' has a considerable historical and sociological interest, if little intrinsic literary value. My aim, then, is not to write an appreciation of the play or to prepare an edition of it, but to inquire into its sources and to determine the form and the stage setting of the foreign operas which it resembles. This investigation will lead up to a study of the form of 'Atis', considered from the point of view of its origin in a musical genre that tended to subordinate dramatic conflict to pageantry and symbolism. In relating the class of plays, usually known as "Haupt- und Staatsaktionen", of which 'Atis' is but a typical example, to their social background, an attempt will be made to study the efforts of seventeenth-century actors to make good the lack of dramatic interest by means of acting, and to offer a more satisfactory explanation of the divorce of the theatre from the drama than would be possible starting from an historical survey of the player-companies. It is hoped at the same time that these investigations will throw new light on the nature and extent of Italian influence on the "Wanderbühne" in the late seventeenth and eighteenth centuries—a subject which for obvious reasons has never received the same attention as the English influence on dramatic production in the earlier part of the seventeenth century.

My sincere thanks are due, and are here gratefully tendered, to the trustees of the Tiarks Fund for the generosity which made the publication of this work possible. To Professor Willoughby I am especially indebted for his valuable criticism of the first draft of my essay, originally planned as the introduction to an edition of the play, and for his remarkable patience with my habits of procrastination; to Geheimrat Professor Oskar Walzel of Bonn for drawing my attention to several omissions and inaccuracies in the final typescript copy; to my friend and former colleague at Newcastle-on-Tyne, Mr F. Austin Child, for indispensable help with the description of the stage designs reproduced in this volume. I should also like to thank the Research Fund Committee of the Queen's University of Belfast for the aid of a grant, without which it would have been difficult to obtain the material necessary for carrying out the researches, also the Authorities of the National Library at Vienna and the Library of the University of Bonn for their assistance and courtesy. Dr Richard Samuel kindly undertook the task of preparing the index, and to him and Mrs Cynthia Crews I am grateful for revising the proofs.

Lastly, I would express my deep sense of gratitude to Professor R. A. Williams, without whose inspiring guidance and unfailing encouragement throughout my work this book would probably never have seen the light.

M. B.

CAMBRIDGE 1938

The National Library at Vienna, formerly known as the Hofbibliothek, contains preserved in manuscript a number of secular plays which resemble, both in content and form, the operas performed at Venice between the years 1637 and 1700. The titles of some fifteen of these plays were mentioned in the year 1889, and detailed synopses of the content of six were given by Carl Heine in a book dealing with the repertoire of the "Wanderbühne"[1] in the latter half of the seventeenth century and during the first three decades of the eighteenth, that is, prior to the reforms of Gottsched in Leipzig.

Heine attempted to prove on very slight evidence that these plays were of Italian or Spanish rather than of English origin, and for one of them 'Der Stumme Prinz Atis' (MS. 13107) he was able to name a probable Italian model. His main argument for the Italian origin of 'Atis' was based upon the assumption of the existence of burlesque scenes that served as a foil to the main plot, in imitation of Italian popular drama. It seemed to me worth while to find out whether the Italian opera 'Creso' of the year 1678 was the original of 'Atis', whether the burlesque scenes described by Heine really existed, and if so, to investigate the exact relation of the German play to its Italian original. An examination of this kind promised to explain not only the type of play chosen by the popular actor-authors in Germany, when English influence had altogether vanished, but also to account for certain modifications made in the original so as to adapt it to the taste of a popular audience.

[1] Carl Heine, *Das Schauspiel der deutschen Wanderbühne*, Halle, 1889. Heine was successively manager of a theatre in Hamburg and of the Deutsches Theater in Berlin.

The existence not only of a German translation of 'Creso'[1] (published as was the Italian libretto at Vienna in 1678), but also of a Hamburg libretto of the year 1684 on the same theme, proved at first somewhat bewildering and seemed likely to complicate considerably the investigations into the origins of 'Atis'. The possibility, however, of rejecting at once the German translation of 1678 as part of the basis of inquiry soon became evident, since it was found to be a word for word and rather uninteresting rendering of the Italian text, displaying no originality whatever. The Hamburg 'Croesus' on the other hand promised to solve certain difficulties; what was of interest here, as compared with the Italian 'Creso', was the existence of comic scenes in each act similar to those contained in the popular play 'Atis' but differing altogether from the comic episodes of the Italian opera, from which both the 'Croesus' and the 'Atis' evidently derived. The similarities between the operas and the 'Atis' in the main spectacular scenes, and the differences between the Italian opera on the one hand and the German opera and German play on the other, in respect of their comic scenes, thus form the points on which all the lines of the present inquiry focus. Before proceeding with the investigations, the general scope of which has been already indicated in the preface, it will be necessary to describe the MS., to discuss the authorship of the play and its provenance and to offer some explanation of the cultivation of Italian opera at Vienna.

[1] This German translation, mentioned by Alexander von Weilen in *Zur Wiener Theatergeschichte*, Schriften des österr. Vereins für Bibliothekswesen, Wien, 1901, p. 23, may be found in the Musikalien-Sammlung of the National-Bibliothek, Vienna. The Hamburg libretto is contained in the *Hamburger Opernsammlung*, vol. I, No. 26, Staatsbibliothek, Hamburg.

CHAPTER I

A. DESCRIPTION OF MS., AUTHORSHIP, DATE, PROVENANCE

B. ITALIAN INFLUENCE ON THE ARTS IN VIENNA

A. *Description of MS., Authorship, Date, Provenance*

The MS. of 'Atis', No. 13107 of the National Library at Vienna, consists of thirty-five closely written quarto sheets, the first of which contains in addition to the title the words: "Hoffmann Direc. Comicus. Ao. 1723 Mense augusto", followed by the dramatis personae, the names of five actors and two lists of properties. The first of the latter is crossed out, the ink being faded and the writing illegible, whilst Frau Neuberin in the chief female rôle is the only player's name that is legible. The last page of the MS. ends with the note: "Finito d. 27ten Mart 1708. M. Dorcheus."

It seems at first difficult to reconcile either of the dates 1708 or 1723 with the presence of the Neuberin in the cast, for the Neubers did not become directors of a touring theatrical company until the 8th August 1727.[1] They did, however, belong, we are told, before the year 1722 to the troupe known as the "Kurfürstlich Sächsische Hofkomödianten" (for which they themselves later received the concession from the Saxon Court), under the management of Johann Caspar Haacke.[2] Haacke, at one time a barber's

[1] F. J. von Reden-Esbeck, *Caroline Neuber und ihre Zeitgenossen. Ein Beitrag zur dt. Kultur- und Theatergesch.* Leipzig, 1881, p. 52.
[2] M. Fürstenau, *Zur Gesch. der Musik und des Theaters am Hof zu Dresden*, Dresden, 1862, vol. II, pp. 310–12; Reden-Esbeck, *op. cit.* pp. 43, 55; cf. Th. Hampe, *Die Entwicklung des Theaterwesens in Nürnberg von der 2. Hälfte des 15. Jahrh. bis 1806*, Nürnberg, 1900, p. 268.

apprentice in Dresden,[1] had joined the Elenson players, a company founded probably about the year 1670 by Andreas Elenson, a native of Vienna. At any rate Elenson, whose wife Maria Margarete was also an actress, appeared between 1671 and 1695 at Graz, Dresden, Vienna, Leipzig and Augsburg.[2] Elenson's son, Julius Franz, who had become the Pantalon in Velten's troupe,[3] married Sophie Julia, a Hamburg actress.[4] Julius Franz died in 1708, and three years later his shrewd and fascinating actress-widow married the above-named Johann Caspar Haacke, then the Harlequin of the Elenson company.[5] Sophie Julia seems either to have enjoyed matrimony as much as acting or to have possessed sound business instincts which enabled her to secure a manager for her company each time the post fell vacant, for she was married a third time, in 1722, to Karl Ludwig Hoffmann, a member of her own troupe,[6] who thus became a joint director of the Elenson-Haacke troupe of players. This must be the Hoffmann, then, whose name appears on the MS. of 'Atis'. The Elenson-Haacke-Hoffmann company was probably in Vienna in 1722, certainly Sophie Julia was there in that year, and Hoffmann's name is to be found in several MSS. which are preserved at the National Library and dated 1722 or 1723. He was evidently still in charge of the same troupe when Gottsched arrived at Leipzig in 1724 and was, as the new dictator of German taste tells us, playing "lauter schwülstige und mit Harlekinslustbarkeiten unter-

[1] W. Flemming, *Das Schauspiel der Wanderbühne*, Dt. Lit. Reihe XIII, Barock, Leipzig, 1931, p. 60; Reden-Esbeck, *op. cit.* p. 44; cf. E. Devrient, *Gesch. der dt. Schauspielkunst*, Leipzig, 1848, vol. I, p. 226.
[2] Alexander von Weilen, "Die Theater Wiens", *Gesch. des Wiener Theaterwesens*, Ges. für vervielfältigende Kunst, Wien, 1899, p. 118; cf. Hampe, *op. cit.* p. 291.
[3] Fürstenau, *op. cit.* vol. II, p. 300; cf. J. F. Schütze, *Hamburgische Theatergesch.* Hamburg, 1794, p. 48.
[4] Flemming, *op. cit.* p. 60.
[5] Flemming, *ibid.* p. 60; cf. Oscar Teuber, *Gesch. des Prager Theaters, Von den Anfängen des Schauspielwesens bis auf die neueste Zeit*, Prag, 1883–88, p. 105.          [6] Teuber, *op. cit.* p. 105.

mengte Haupt- und Staatsaktionen"[1] there during the Leipzig fair.

In all probability Hoffmann took down the play 'Atis' from a copy belonging to the rival Velten company, for the Dorcheus mentioned on the last page of the MS. may have been the actor Dorscheus or Dorseus, the 'Pickle Herring' of Frau Velten's troupe, who, according to Fürstenau, later graduated at Vienna and had some knowledge of chemistry.[2] The play may, therefore, have been originally on the repertoire of the Velten troupe. We are told that both the Velten and Haacke-Elenson companies were in Frankfurt am Main in 1711 for the coronation of Charles VI, and that Frau Velten, being no match there for her astute rival, Sophie Julia, was unable to keep her troupe together, so that half of the members deserted her and went over to the successful rival company.[3] Dorcheus may easily have been one of the deserters. It is not necessary to assume that he was the author of 'Atis', indeed it is more probable that he only made a copy of a play which was on Velten's repertoire.

Nothing definite is known of the early performances of 'Atis'. Johannes Meissner mentions it in his list of comedies under the title 'Der von Ciro gefangene Crösus, dessen Freiheit', which would indicate that it must have existed about the year 1700, or at any rate between that date and 1710.[4] 'Der Stumme Prinz Atis' has no connection whatever, as Nagl and Zeidler's history of Austrian literature[5] suggests, with the 'Athys' written in 1673 by the Benedictine monk, Simon Rettenpacher, for a special performance at the university of Salzburg. The subject of Rettenpacher's play is the slaying of Athys, son of Croesus, by Adrastes, whereas in the popular play the hero is the dumb son who suddenly

[1] Reden-Esbeck, *op. cit.* p. 47.
[2] Fürstenau, *op. cit.* vol. II, p. 300.
[3] Teuber, *op. cit.* p. 105.
[4] J. Meissner, "Die englischen Komödianten in Österreich", *Jahrb. der Shakespeare Ges.* vol. XIX, p. 152, No. 134.
[5] Vol. I, p. 742.

regained his speech in a battle between the Lydians and Persians.[1]

'Atis' is an adaptation in prose of 'Creso', an Italian opera, which, as is evident from the title-page of its libretto, was performed in the year 1678 by command of the Emperor Leopold I to celebrate the birthday of his third wife, Eleonora Magdalene Theresia (Eleonora von Pfalz-Neuburg). The words were written by Count Niccolo Minato, the most prolific librettist of his time. A native of Bergamo, he was Court poet at Vienna for no less than twenty-nine years, from 1669 to 1698.[2] The music of the opera was by Antonio Draghi, a gifted dramatic composer who was born at Ferrara in 1635 and invited to Vienna in 1664, where he was apparently not in the employment of the Emperor Leopold himself but of the Dowager Empress Eleonora.[3] Later he was placed in charge of the music at the Imperial Court and was musical director there from 1682 to 1700.[4] Like Minato he was most productive, as may be seen from the list of his works performed at the Court in Vienna, the number of his operas alone amounting to no fewer than sixty-seven. Thus Minato and Draghi were at the Imperial Court at the same time.

B. *Italian Influence on the Arts in Vienna*

But some explanation must be given here of the predominance of Italian influence upon the development of the arts in Vienna. In inviting Italians to his Court Leopold was but following in the footsteps of his predecessors. Italian music,

[1] Arthur Kutscher, *Das Salzburger Barocktheater*, Wien-Leipzig-München, 1924, p. 118; cf. Flemming, *Das Ordensdrama*, Dt. Lit. Reihe XIII, Barock, Leipzig, 1930, p. 32; Rettenpacher, Ord. S. Benedicti Monachi Cremifanensis in Austria Superiore (Kremsmünster), *Selecta Dramata diversis temporibus conscripta et in scena recitata*, Salisburgi, Jan Bapt. Mayr. 1683.

[2] R. von Kralik, *Gesch. der Stadt Wien*, Wien, 1926, p. 216; cf. v. Weilen, *op. cit.* p. 71.

[3] Kralik, *op. cit.* p. 207.

[4] v. Weilen, *op. cit.* p. 71.

art and literature had for generations been cultivated by the Hapsburgs. As early as 1493 Maximilian I had called scholars from Italy to the university of Vienna, and for musical entertainments at Court he had kept his own private orchestra which was distinctly international in character, the Italian element, however, far outweighing all the others.[1] The private orchestra became a regular tradition at the Court, it grew in size with each of the successors of Maximilian and the music was invariably in charge of an Italian. The preference for Italian art may to some extent be explained by the frequent intermarriages between the Austrian and Italian ruling houses. In 1494 Maximilian I married a daughter of the Duke of Milan,[2] and the wife of Duke Ferdinand of Tyrol, younger brother of the Emperor Maximilian II, was a daughter of Duke William of Mantua.[3] Eleonora, the second wife of Ferdinand II, was also a Mantuan princess, in fact the daughter of Duke Vincenzo Gonzaga,[4] famous as one of the leading managers of the Mask Comedies and patron of the arts in Italy. In Ferdinand II's reign Italian even became the official language of the Austrian Court.[5] Not only Mantuan but Tuscan princesses found their way to Austria. Claudia de' Medici married the Archduke Leopold V of Tyrol and twenty years later another Tuscan princess, Anne de' Medici, became the wife of the Archduke Ferdinand Charles.[6] Their daughter, Claudia Felicitas, a great lover of Italian music, became the Holy Roman Empress in the days of Leopold I. And if a Hapsburg monarch required the sanction of tradition for installing foreigners in the important positions that he had to offer, Leopold had but to look back to his ancestor Ferdinand III, who not only founded an Italian academy of letters in his capital but

[1] F. Biach-Schiffmann, *Giovanni und Ludovico Burnacini*, Wien-Berlin, 1931, p. 10.
[2] v. Weilen, *op. cit.* p. 44.
[3] Marcus Landau, *Die ital. Lit. am österr. Hofe*, Wien, 1879, p. 8.
[4] Landau, *ibid.* p. 8.
[5] v. Weilen, *op. cit.* p. 45.   [6] v. Weilen, *ibid.* p. 45.

invited during his reign several celebrated foreign artists, the chief of these being Johann Wilhelm Baur, miniature painter and etcher, and the architect and stage designer, Giovanni Burnacini. Baur was, it is true, not an Italian but a native of Strassburg. He had, however, worked six years in Italy prior to 1637 when he became Court painter at Vienna.[1] Ferdinand III's third wife, also an Eleonora of Mantua, is generally supposed to have suggested to the Emperor the idea of engaging Giovanni Burnacini,[2] and certainly the beginning of his activity in Vienna coincides with the date of her marriage to Ferdinand.[3] Though the rôle played by Baur in the development of Baroque art has never been satisfactorily investigated, it is certain that he exercised a profound influence on Ludovico Burnacini, son of the above-named Giovanni who at a very early age accompanied his father to Vienna as his apprentice in the year 1651 and later designed the stage setting and the scenery for at least a hundred and fifteen operas (and probably many more) that were performed at the Court of the Hapsburgs during the second half of the seventeenth century.[4]

Italian influence on art and literature being so pronounced at the Imperial Court, it is hardly surprising to find that an opera developed in Vienna which not only from a musical and literary point of view but from the standpoint of its complicated stage technique is the offspring of Italian opera. Indeed, no sooner did a new type of musical entertainment make its appearance in Italy in the early seventeenth century than the Imperial Court secured the services of the three master-composers of the new Venetian school, Cavalli, whose real name was Caletti Bruni, Marc Antonio Cesti and the elder Ziani.[5] Though all three composers attracted attention

[1] Biach-Schiffmann, *op. cit.* p. 11.
[2] Eduard Vehse, *Gesch. der dt. Höfe seit der Reformation*, Hamburg, 1852, Part IV, Gesch. des österr. Hofes, p. 320.
[3] Biach-Schiffmann, *op. cit.* p. 21.     [4] Biach-Schiffmann, *ibid.* p. 47.
[5] H. Kretzschmar, *Gesch. der Oper*, Leipzig, 1919, p. 137; cf. R. Lach, "Wien als Musikstadt", *Wien, sein Boden und seine Gesch.* Wien, 1924, p. 409.

in their time and are still of some importance in the history of opera, they do not concern us here, for it was not they but Minato who fixed the form of the Italian libretto. He was the most characteristic product of Venetian influence and seems to have enjoyed undisputed authority amongst the writers and composers of his time. But the text of a seventeenth-century Italian opera is of minor importance as compared with its "mise-en-scène". Since in fact the words were intended to be accompanied and enhanced by music and were written obviously with a view to the total impression to be produced upon the audience as a result of the combination of certain musical, pictorial and architectural effects, no account of the Venetian Baroque opera could be complete without some account, however inexhaustive, of the design of the stage, the scenery and the general decorative scheme of the whole setting of the opera.

The second chapter will, therefore, be devoted to an inquiry into the origin and development of the Venetian opera, followed by an examination of its structural elements, as laid down by Minato, and an attempt will be made in Chapter III to deal with the "mise-en-scène" of the particular variety of Baroque opera that depended for its success upon the designing ability of the two Burnacini. As the opera had a successful rival at Vienna in the Jesuit drama, it will be necessary to consider in the concluding section of the third chapter the nature of the relation between these two similar types of theatrical performances, before proceeding to an investigation of the popular theatre at Vienna and its dependence upon the opera.

## CHAPTER II

### *Origin and Structural Elements of the Venetian Opera*

The man who is usually considered to be the originator of the new type of musical drama that became popular in Venice in the thirties of the seventeenth century and was known as the Venetian opera, was the composer Claudio Monteverde, a native of Cremona. It seems to me, however, that what Monteverde introduced into the new entertainment was a dramatic and human element[1] which was almost consistently neglected by those who succeeded him, and that his opera is, therefore, not typically Venetian at all. Monteverde, who had been musical director at the Court of the Gonzaga in Mantua from 1604 to 1613, was appointed "chapelmaster" at St Mark's in Venice in the latter year.[2] His first important opera, 'Orfeo', was produced at the carnival in Mantua in the year 1607, first on the stage of the "Accademia degl' In vaghiti" and later before the Court.[3] 'Orfeo' is the story of the love of Orpheus for Eurydice and its tragic ending. In choosing a subject taken from the ancient world, Monteverde was but following the example set by a group of young scholars who met regularly in Florence at the home of Giovanni Bardi, Count of Vernio, a patron of the arts and a man of wide learning. Their aim was to cultivate literature, music and the sciences, and realizing the place and importance of music in ancient tragedy they decided to imitate the Greeks.[4] What was new in Monteverde's 'Orfeo' was that the music, apart altogether from the words, was the sincere and passionate expression of the composer's grief at the loss

[1] C. Hubert H. Parry, *Oxford Hist. of Music*, vol. III, pp. 135, 176.
[2] Kretzschmar, *op. cit.* p. 55.
[3] Kretzschmar, *ibid.* p. 55.
[4] G. B. Doni, *Della musica scenica*, Firenze, 1763, chap. 9.

8

of his own wife.[1] Instrumental music became more than a mere accompaniment of words, the orchestra interpreting the feelings of the characters directly and the libretto being subordinated to the music.[2] In reality this was contrary to the intention of the Florentine school which aimed at intensifying the effect of the words by means of the music,[3] thus enhancing the meaning of a poem.

One of the chief members of the enterprising fraternity at Florence that was bent upon solving the problems of theatrical representation accompanied by instruments, was Ottavio Rinuccini, a poet who, though not himself a composer, was able, by reason of his cultivated taste in music and his deep appreciation of it,[4] to give valuable assistance to musicians like Monteverde. Rinuccini wrote a play entitled 'Dafne'[5] and persuaded the composer Giacomo Peri to set it to music. Doni, a contemporary of Rinuccini and author of a treatise on ancient Greek music, describes 'Dafne' as a "favola boschereccia", that is, a shepherd play, and tells us that it was the first drama ("Azione") written in the new musical style. It was performed at Florence, probably in the year 1594,[6] in the house of Jacopo Corsi who in virtue of his interest in everything pertaining to the muses had succeeded the above-mentioned Bardi as patron of the fraternity. 'Dafne' was followed in 1600 by Rinuccini's 'Euridice', performed at Florence to celebrate the marriage of Marie de' Medici with Henry IV of France.[7] In 1607 Rinuccini dramatized the story of Theseus and Ariadne and the opera 'Arianna' was

[1] Lacy Collison-Morley, *Italy after the Renaissance*, London, 1930, p. 84.
[2] Collison-Morley, *ibid.* p. 84.
[3] Kretzschmar, *op. cit.* p. 23, and v. Weilen, *op. cit.* p. 56.
[4] Doni, *op. cit.*; see Kretzschmar, *op. cit.* p. 19.
[5] 'Dafne', adapted by Martin Opitz and set to the music of Heinrich Schütz, was performed at Torgau in 1627 during the wedding festivities of the Saxon princess, Luise. This was the first German opera of any importance. See Kretzschmar, *op. cit.* p. 136; cf. Schiedermair, *Die deutsche Oper*, Leipzig, 1930, p. 20.
[6] Kretzschmar, *op. cit.* p. 31.
[7] Kretzschmar, *ibid.* p. 31.

performed at a royal wedding in Mantua in 1607, the music having been contributed by none other than Monteverde,[1] whom we already know as the composer of 'Orfeo'.

The names Orpheus, Eurydice and Daphne at once suggest the pastoral, and indeed the Florentine "operas" resemble earlier pastoral plays not only in their subjects and their scenery, but like them they seem to have been intended for performance on the stages of the numerous Court theatres throughout Italy. Since the pastoral play was the favourite entertainment at Court, it is easy to explain Rinuccini's choice of this form for his libretti. Tasso's 'Aminta' was performed at the Belvedere palace of the Duke of Ferrara, the whole Court being in attendance,[2] whilst the earliest of the pastoral dramas, Politian's 'Orfeo', was written specially in 1471 for Cardinal Francesco Gonzaga of Mantua,[3] and in his 'Euridice' Rinuccini adopted many of the characters, indeed even many of the verses, of his predecessor.[4]

One of the main features of the plot of the Florentine operas like 'Dafne' and 'Euridice' was a complicated love intrigue in which several pairs of lovers were presented. A similar love intrigue occurs in many pastoral plays, for example, in Agostino Beccari's 'Sacrifizio', acted at Ferrara in 1554,[5] where the fortunes of no fewer than three pairs of lovers are involved; in Agostino Argenti's 'Lo Sfortunato' of the year 1567[6] and in Guarini's 'Pastor Fido' produced in 1590.[7]

But Rinuccini did not choose the pastoral form merely for the sake of pleasing the Italian aristocracy.[8] From a purely musical point of view his choice was calculated to

[1] Kretzschmar, *op. cit.* p. 62; cf. Parry, *op. cit.* p. 50.

[2] Louis E. Lord, *The Orpheus of Politian and the Aminta of Tasso*, Oxford, 1931, p. 62.

[3] Lord, *ibid.* p. 70; cf. W. W. Greg, *Pastoral Poetry and Pastoral Drama*, London, 1905, p. 157.

[4] Kretzschmar, *op. cit.* p. 34.

[5] Lord, *op. cit.* p. 59; cf. Greg, *op. cit.* p. 174.

[6] Lord, *op. cit.* p. 60.

[7] Lord, *ibid.* p. 65.        [8] Kretzschmar, *op. cit.* p. 43.

ensure the greatest degree of success, for Italians had since the middle of the sixteenth century been familiar with the madrigal, that is to say, with the scenery of pastoral poetry and the emotions which it expresses.[1] The schools of music in Italy from 1500 on had cultivated the Neapolitan "Villanella", a type of music that was extremely popular and a direct descendant of the madrigal.[2] Moreover, it is interesting to note that the libretto of Monteverde's 'Orfeo' was written by Alessandro Striggio, the son of the famous madrigalist of the same name.[3] The two most significant features of the Florentine operas were, then, that they were pastoral in character and intended for performance on the stages of the Court theatres.

With the appearance of 'Orfeo' and 'Arianna', Monteverde became the foremost representative of the dramatic music of his time, and the city that adopted him was soon to gain an important place in the history of opera. It is significant that Venice was unlike other Italian cities in having no Court, so that a new theatre established at St Cassian in 1637 had nothing to fear from the rival performances of the aristocracy. The Teatro di San Cassiano was the first public opera-house to exist in Europe. No fewer than thirty-seven different operas were produced here between 1637 and 1700.[4] Seven other opera-houses were founded between 1639 and 1677, and before the end of the century some three hundred operas were composed for the Venetian theatres and almost as many found their way to other Italian cities and to the various Courts of Germany, particularly Munich, Dresden and Vienna;[5] a sufficient testimony not only to the readiness with which the Venetians received the new entertainment, but also to the growing enthusiasm for the opera in Germany.

The Venetian opera was a form of melodrama set to music. The hero of this musical drama was usually a ruler who had

---

[1] Kretzschmar, *ibid.* p. 43.  
[3] Kretzschmar, *ibid.* p. 55.  
[5] Kretzschmar, *ibid.* p. 83.

[2] Kretzschmar, *ibid.* p. 43.  
[4] Kretzschmar, *ibid.* p. 82.

been dethroned or banished or defeated in battle by his enemy, and an important part of the plot was an intrigue carried on by some prince for the purpose of usurping the royal power. This gave an opportunity to present Court scenes of great pomp and splendour; we have what in fact in German would be called a "Haupt- und Staatsaktion". The plot, an account of which was usually given in the preface, was supposed to be based upon historical facts, the so-called "fatti storici" which were combined with political intrigues invented by the poet, termed the "accidenti verissimi",[1] and the play was still incomplete without the series of complicated love intrigues characteristic of the Florentine opera, interspersed with playful scenes depicting bucolic life.

A further important feature and perhaps the most popular part of the performances in Venice was a humorous intermezzo, a short musical interlude which had developed from the madrigal. It was at first intended as an imitation of the Greek Satyr plays, but later developed more and more along the lines of the impromptu comedy, and as such was forerunner of the later opera bouffe.[2] A very early example of this type of madrigal-intermezzo is the 'Amfiparnasso' of Orazio Vecchi, probably performed at Modena in 1594, though not printed till 1604.[3] The central figure, a foolish old lover, Pantalon, appears accompanied by two servants who provide a number of extremely farcical scenes. It is significant that the comic scenes should have been introduced at Venice though not surprising, since in the absence of Court patrons it was necessary to please a public that paid for the seats.[4]

The pastoral drama with all its artificial adjuncts was an important source of the Venetian opera. The more stereotyped in form the opera became, the more did it tend to suppress the human interest introduced by the genius of Monteverde and to develop the ornamental accessories that it had borrowed from the pastoral play. In extinguishing the

---

[1] Kretzschmar, *op. cit.* p. 85.     [2] Kretzschmar, *ibid.* p. 27.
[3] Kretzschmar, *ibid.* p. 28.     [4] Collison-Morley, *op. cit.* p. 85.

dramatic element and replacing it by purely theatrical effects, it was but pandering to the taste for display so prevalent in the Baroque age. But this does not mean that the opera completely lost touch with the real life of ordinary people, for where the comic element prevailed as at Venice, the opera approximated to some extent to the impromptu comedy. Contact was thus established with the life of the burgher, and this human interest must have counterbalanced in some degree the artificial atmosphere of the opera, especially where the actor found scope to ridicule Court conventions and mannerisms or to mock Authority. Even at Vienna this comic element does not entirely disappear, though it was subordinate to the main aim which the Viennese librettists kept before their minds—the glorification of the Hapsburgs.

The Venetian opera, deriving as it did from the pastoral, had from the beginning of its development a certain atmosphere of unreality, indeed of artificiality. Far from being an imitation of Greek drama, as the Florentine poets had intended it to be, it faithfully reproduced the complicated political and social life of Italy in the sixteenth and seventeenth centuries. The names given to the heroes are to be found in ancient poetry and history, but the chief characters themselves are Italians—usurpers, banished rulers and pretenders to the throne. Thus the opera reproduces contemporary life and manners with all their conventionality and affectation. In this sense it is true to say that it surrenders more and more, as it develops, to the impromptu comedy which was already in a state of deterioration. The opera had a stereotyped form and followed a scheme acceptable to the Court. Histrionic and dramatic elements were gradually suppressed to allow stage effect to predominate. The next chapter will explain how the opera in Vienna moved farther and farther away from actual contact with life and became a grand pageant that appealed to the senses rather than to the imagination of the audience.

CHAPTER III

## A. THE "MISE-EN-SCÈNE" OF THE VENETIAN OPERA

## B. THE JESUIT DRAMA AND THE OPERA AT VIENNA

### A. *The "Mise-en-Scène" of the Venetian Opera*

It is difficult to obtain accurate information about the actual "machinery" employed on the Italian stage to produce the magnificent stage effects that gradually became the chief feature, not only of all the performances of the aristocracy, but also of the opera at Venice. Giacomo Torelli, an Italian architect and artist born at Fano in 1608, is said to have invented the mechanism for bringing about rapid changes of scenery and decoration; it was for this very reason that he was known in his own time as the "Great Magician".[1] One of the main reasons for the lack of actual details is due to the careful way in which the masters of the new technique guarded their secret. A certain amount of information is, however, available from descriptions given by Torelli's contemporaries, particularly by Josef Furttenbach, a German

---

[1] The credit of invention can scarcely be ascribed to Torelli. The most one can say is that he was reviving an earlier custom, for Leonardo da Vinci made use of strange mechanical devices in the festival known as "Il Paradiso" in 1489, on the occasion of the entry into Milan of its Duke, Gian Galeazzo, with his wife, Isabella of Aragon. (See Enid Welsford, *The Court Masque*, Cambridge, 1927, p. 87.) Leonardo was familiar with the tradition of the great Florentine festival processions, a special feature of which was the ascent or descent of celestial beings in clouds (*ibid.* p. 82). The artist Cecca is said to have invented the "clouds" that were borne in the procession (*ibid.* p. 83), and Cecca himself had a forerunner in the Florentine architect Brunelleschi who, at the beginning of the fifteenth century, attempted to revive the complicated machinery of the ancient Greek stage. (See J. A. Symonds, *Renaissance in Italy. Italian Literature*, vol. I, pp. 318, 319.)

architect and mathematician, who travelled extensively in Italy between 1612 and 1622.[1] From these it would seem that the opera aimed at startling the audience by means of sudden and miraculous transformations, the action taking place now on the earth or again in heaven or in the air or sea, the Gods and Tritons or even the signs of the Zodiac appearing as the actors.[2] We are told that Italians were accustomed to seeing on the stage life-size elephants, live camels, chariots drawn by wild beasts, dancing horses,[3] machines flying through the air;[4] that dragons' teeth suddenly changed into armed men; that the very heavens opened and the Gods appeared and that the orchestra was borne down from heaven upon the clouds.[5]

It was undoubtedly because of its unusual splendour that the Venetian opera found favour with the Hapsburg monarchs, for the tendency of the Austrian Court, and in this respect it did not differ from others, was to assimilate its great theatrical functions to those of Louis XIV's Court.[6] It is scarcely possible to estimate with any degree of accuracy the extent of French influence upon performances at Vienna or the exact nature of the relation existing between the Court pageants in France and Italy. Certain it is that Cavalli, whom we have already mentioned, wrote at least two operas for the French Court.[7] But long before his time, under Francis I, Italian influence had begun to make itself felt in the French capital. Mazarin engaged Italian artists in 1645, amongst others the "Magician", Giacomo Torelli,[8] who was given the Petit Bourbon Theatre. On the other hand, it must not be forgotten that Rinuccini had been at the Courts of Henry IV and Marie de' Medici, and it was

---

[1] Josef Furttenbach, *Architectura recreationis*, Augsburg, 1640; cf. Biach, Schiffmann, *op. cit.* p. 15.

[2] Kretzschmar, *op. cit.* p. 45.

[3] Collison-Morley, *op. cit.* p. 85.

[4] John Evelyn, *The Diary and Correspondence*, ed. by Will Bray, p. 137.

[5] Kretzschmar, *op. cit.* p. 46.     [6] Parry, *op. cit.* p. 174.

[7] Kretzschmar, *op. cit.* p. 99.     [8] Biach-Schiffmann, *op. cit.* p. 11.

probably he who first introduced the elaborate French ballet to Italy.[1] This form of entertainment enjoyed an unprecedented popularity at Vienna, and its influence was tending to cause the opera to develop not so much along the lines of a musical drama as of a great Court pageant in honour of Hymen.

It may well have been Giovanni Burnacini who brought into use in Vienna the elaborate architecture and the miraculous equipment of the Italian stage. Whereas the machinery must remain a matter of conjecture, a fairly correct idea of the actual stage and general setting of the operas may be formed from a number of printed texts that are preserved in the musical section of the National Library at Vienna. These contain not only detailed descriptions of the theatre and stage, together with elaborate stage directions, but many engravings of the proscenium and of the interior of the stage as it appeared for the different scenes.[2] The engravings, however, do not always make clear the comparative relation of architectural and plastic features on the one hand and painted scenery on the other, but it is fairly safe to assume that in this respect, as in others, the Burnacini at Vienna followed the tradition of the Italian stage. The ideal of the Baroque architects was the perspective scene of great depth, and for this plastic decoration was allied with painted scenery calculated to produce an illusion of reality. Ample proof of that may be found in the descriptions of Furttenbach and in later Italian works.[3] Very little is known of the Burnacini except that both father and son entered the

[1] Biach-Schiffmann, *op. cit.* p. 11. The French ballet itself was indebted to the Italian revels and its inventor was an Italian. See Welsford, *op. cit.* p. 110.

[2] Alex. v. Weilen drew attention to these in his history of the theatres at Vienna, and Frau Biach-Schiffmann has included in her study of the Burnacini a selection of descriptions taken from the texts with the engravings to which they refer.

[3] Nicola Sabbattini, *Anleitung, Dekorationen u. Theatermaschinen herzustellen,* 1639, ed. by Willi Flemming, Weimar, 1926; Fabricio C. Motta, *Trattato sopra la struttura de' teatri e scene,* Guastallo, 1676.

service of the Austrian Court in 1651,[1] under Ferdinand III, that Giovanni built a theatre in Vienna for the Emperor in the following year,[2] and that he was in charge of the theatrical entertainment at Ratisbon in 1653 during the session of the Reichstag. Giovanni designed the stage and scenery for 'La Gara', the first of the grand operas performed in his new theatre in 1652. The printed libretto of this opera, together with its five engravings, is invaluable for a study of the opera at that time. Giovanni may have been directly influenced by the opera at Venice. Certainly both he and his brother, Marc Antonio, likewise an architect, seem to have had some intimate connection with the city of lagoons. Marc Antonio proceeded direct from Venice to Vienna[3] and an engraving, bearing the name Giovanni Burnacini in the National Library at Paris, is dated Venice 30th August 1642.[4] Further, in the dedication of the text of an opera of the 24th January 1651, he states that he had been working in Venice for some time.[5] Since he even had a theatre of his own in that city,[6] it is reasonable to suppose that he played an important rôle as Italian stage designer before going to Austria at all, and he must have been acquainted with Giacomo Torelli prior to the latter's departure for Paris on the invitation of Mazarin.[7]

The great Court operas that began with 'La Gara' were performed by imperial command to celebrate events of importance in the royal household, such as weddings, births and anniversaries. Their main aim was to emphasize the power of the Empire and the absolute authority of its Head. Since Giovanni Burnacini's descriptions in the preface of 'La Gara' make that point clearer than anything else could, it will be worth while quoting at length from them:

On the appearance of his Majesty with the other princes of the Royal House, the trumpets are sounded, the trumpeters move

[1] Biach-Schiffmann, *op. cit.* p. 30.    [2] Biach-Schiffmann, *ibid.* p. 38.
[3] Biach-Schiffmann, *ibid.* p. 33.    [4] Biach-Schiffmann, *ibid.* p. 30.
[5] Biach-Schiffmann, *ibid.* p. 29.
[6] R. Haas, *Die Wiener Oper*, Wien-Budapest, 1926, p. 2.
[7] Biach-Schiffmann, *op. cit.* p. 48.

towards the throne of Their Majesties and take up their positions. The double-throne which is erected at the centre back of the theatre opposite the proscenium is approached by five steps and surrounded by a finely wrought balustrade. At each of the two corners of the top step a female figure, larger than life-size, is erected upon a pedestal, one representing Peace, the other Virtue. These figures support a richly wrought canopy over their Majesties' Heads....[1] In keeping with the splendour of the throne is the arcaded amphitheatre stretching in a semi-circle and reaching the soffits, with its two galleries for the ladies and cavaliers of the court.[2] The galleries are elegantly adorned with two tiers of columns, the lower ones Doric, the upper ones Ionic.

As was mentioned above, the libretto of 'La Gara' contains five engravings representing the stage and the proscenium. From these it may be seen that the latter was formed of four Corinthian piers at either side, the shafts being double-ranked and decorated with fielded panels of varied design. The piers rested upon a plain stage front and had a full entablature which formed the top of the proscenium opening, bearing in the centre the double eagle on a cartouche. The outer oval ring of this was supported by an angel on either side and the whole was surmounted by the crown. Swags from the base of the cartouche were connected to the soffit of the entablature and bore musical trophies. Over the capitals on either side perched the eagle with wings outstretched and each foot gripping the abacus of the capital.[3] But, however elaborate this early theatre of Giovanni Burnacini may have been,[4] it was far surpassed in splendour by the Comödiehauss,[5] built in 1666 by his son Ludovico, completed in the following year and opened in 1668 with a performance of one of the most magnificent of Venetian operas, 'Il Pomo d' Oro'. Nowhere is stage effect so imposing as in this opera written in 1666 by Antonio Cesti[6] to celebrate the first

[1] Biach-Schiffmann, *op. cit.* p. 35.    [2] Biach-Schiffmann, *ibid.* p. 35.
[3] Biach-Schiffmann, *ibid.* p. 34.    [4] Its site is not even known to-day.
[5] The Comödiehauss occupied the present site of the National-Bibliothek in the Josefsplatz. See Biach-Schiffmann, *op. cit.* p. 52.
[6] The music was by Francesco Sbarra. See Kretzschmar, *op. cit.* p. 101; cf. v. Kralik, *op. cit.* p. 217.

PLATE II

*'La Gara.' Interior of the Theatre. Tournament Scene*

marriage of Leopold I with the Infanta Margaret Elizabeth of Spain. The staging alone is said to have cost a hundred thousand Reichstaler[1] and the pageantry was more striking than anything ever seen at Mantua, Rome or Naples. Full details of the stage architecture and the "mise-en-scène" are available in the text of the libretto at the National Library in Vienna and in the engravings done by Matthäus Küsel and Franz Geffels from the original designs of Ludovico Burnacini.[2] An attempt will be made to describe three of these engravings, representing respectively the proscenium, the interior of the theatre and the stage during the first scene. The proscenium for the 'Golden Apple' was the same as that used in 1674 for 'Il Fuoco Eterno Custodito dalle Vestali',[3] an opera which celebrated the birth of a daughter to Leopold and Claudia Felicitas of Tyrol whom he had married in 1673 (Margaret Elizabeth had died that very year).[4] Ludovico's treatment of the proscenium is more imaginative and certainly more complicated and bewildering than anything that was ever conceived by his father. The intention is everywhere evident; it is to extol the House of Hapsburg and Hymen. The description given in the dedication page of the libretto is as follows:

Cherubs and winged cherub heads decorate the projecting pilasters of the attic and the spaces between these members are filled with allegorical figures. At the head of the figures are shimmering cartouches surrounded by rich pleated ornament. In the interior of the theatre to the right of the stage and separated from it by the curtain which is raised,[5] there are two strongly veined columns with composite capitals. Between these at the right, on a high pedestal, decorated with shells and scrolls, an allegorical female figure bearing a staff round which coils a

---

[1] Landau, *op. cit.* p. 17; cf. Biach-Schiffmann, *op. cit.* p. 53.
[2] *Ibid.* p. 52.     [3] *Ibid.* pp. 53, 55.     [4] *Ibid.* p. 27.
[5] For the curtain see frontispiece. It depicts a scene in the clouds where Pallas Athene defeats the enemy powers of Discord, Confusion, Hatred and Anger. The Goddess is complete with helmet and spear and carries a shield with a Gorgon's head. On the upper part of the curtain is an angel blowing the trumpet of victory. The flag attached to the trumpet bears the inscription: Cadent a latere tuo.

serpent and a shield with a Medusa head. On the left, corresponding to this, a male figure leans on a club, his arm caught in the coils of a serpent. A second projecting pair of columns, in which is placed a winged female figure with a Medusa head on her breast, her arms indicating great agitation, affords a view of a colonnade. The pedestal on which the figure stands is ornamented with cartouches and cherubs. The corresponding female figure on the left carries a laurel wreath, palm branch and staff with the serpent coils. The columns and the pedestals with the figures placed on them rest upon a high stage front with projecting consoles which are decorated with wreaths of acanthus and fruits. Between the consoles cartouches project in relief. On the projecting consoles, in front of the columns, and situated below the figures described above, are three female figures holding emblems in their hands. The figure nearest the stage on the left grasps a truncated column. Above the columns is a deep entablature with elaborate cartouches and an attic connecting the two sides of the proscenium. This attic merges into an intricate decoration over the stage opening, the soffit of which takes the form of a cambered arch. In the centre is a cartouche on fluttering lambrequins; immediately beneath this is the Austrian double-eagle against a background of light-coloured drapery ending in trophies. The drapery is held in position at each side by one cherub, whilst another, riding on an eagle's back, supports within the framework of a wreath of laurels the initial L (Leopold), the corresponding M (Margaret) appearing on the opposite side, likewise supported by a cherub on the back of an eagle.[1]

Judging by this description, the opera was definitely a pageant in honour of Hymen.

But the engraving which represents the interior of the stage during the first scene is by no means less interesting, for it is the apotheosis of the victorious Leopold himself.[2] Here two Corinthian colonnades appear in perspective and end in a hemicycle. The columns are coupled and decorated with leaves, the capitals showing both Ionic and Corinthian features. Between them are placed the equestrian statues of the Austrian monarchs, all the horses being in prancing attitudes. The fronts of the bases of the statues are rounded

---

[1] Biach-Schiffmann, *op. cit.* p. 99. See Plates I and III. Plate III shows the Court in attendance at the performance with Leopold and Margaret seated in the centre of the dais. The magnificent ceiling is the work of Ludovico Burnacini.      [2] See Plate IV.

PLATE III

'Il Pomo d' Oro.' Interior of the Theatre

PLATE IV

*'Il Pomo d' Oro.'* "*Schaubinne des Österreichischen Ehrn-Ruhms.*" *Prologue*

and decorated with trophies. The strongly modelled entablature recedes between each pair of columns and the recession is marked by a decoration of trophies. A central feature of piled trophies stands in front of the hemicycle, and upon this is placed an equestrian statue representing none other than Leopold himself. Like the other rulers depicted at the sides he wears a crown and wields in his left hand the sceptre, while with the right, which is invisible, he keeps a tight rein on the rearing horse. Two cherubs, one on either side of the main feature of the colonnade, hold above the Monarch a colossal laurel wreath above which hovers the Austrian Glory with crown, shield and fluttering ribbons and mounted upon a Pegasus. In the clouds on one side Amor, on the other Hymen. Surmounting the entablature of the hemicycle are cherubs, and winged cherubs holding laurel wreaths and palm branches are placed on the entablature of the widening colonnades directly over the columns. Near the bases of the equestrian statues stand female figures, impersonating in appropriate costumes, the various countries within the Holy Roman Empire.

Bearing in mind the polychrom effect of Baroque architecture, only a little effort of the imagination is now required to complete the lavish and dazzling picture that a Viennese opera must have presented to the entranced gaze of the spectator. And indeed no opera of the age shows more clearly than does the 'Golden Apple' the general development since Monteverde. The whole emphasis is laid upon the "mise-en-scène". For example, the fourth act shows an earthquake which causes the statue of Venus to tumble down—a subject which might have afforded special scope to the composer. Yet we are told by a musical authority that the music here has nothing particular to say about the earthquake.[1]

From the point of view of pageantry the greatest of all the operas at Vienna was 'La Monarchia Latina Trionfante', the work of Minato, Draghi and Ludovico Burnacini. It

[1] Parry, *op. cit.* p. 175.

was staged in 1678 on the occasion of the birth of the heir to the throne, Joseph.[1] The title itself is a good indication of the subject. The earth accuses at Jupiter's throne the enemy powers, Idleness, Lust for Power, Anger, Hatred and Confusion, whereupon the Gods decide to examine the various ages of humanity and to re-establish the most peaceful government that has hitherto existed. Saturn calls up the four great monarchies of the world and Discord involves them in hostilities in which the Gods themselves take part. The leaders are Minos, Darius, Alexander and Caesar, but it is Caesar who finally emerges triumphant. The Roman Empire is, therefore, re-established and Leopold I is fêted as its most recent representative.[2] In the stage directions given for the Prologue in the libretto we are told that the figure of Joyfulness appeared in front of the curtain which depicted Jupiter mounted on the eagle, hurling his thunderbolts, as well as the fall of the Giants, and that after proclaiming the birth of the heir to the Roman Empire, the figure was carried up as though upon the clouds, with the curtain, as it rose, displaying a vast company of armed men and a procession of elephants advancing towards the front of the stage.[3] Thus the Giants and Jupiter himself disappeared to make way for the Roman Emperor. The private theatre of the Procurator Contarina at Venice with all its lavish display could not have surpassed that of Leopold's Court. But the reader will be able to form a better idea of these scenic splendours than could be given by any description from the few illustrations that have been included in this volume. The selection has been made not so much with a view to throwing light on the historical development of the opera as with the intention of relating it to its cultural background. A selection that is more comprehensive and at the same time chronological will be found in Frau Biach-Schiffmann's study of the Burnacini.

[1] v. Weilen, *op. cit.* p. 66.
[2] Biach-Schiffmann, *op. cit.* p. 59; cf. v. Weilen, *op. cit.* p. 66.
[3] Biach-Schiffmann, *op. cit.* p. 118.

PLATE V

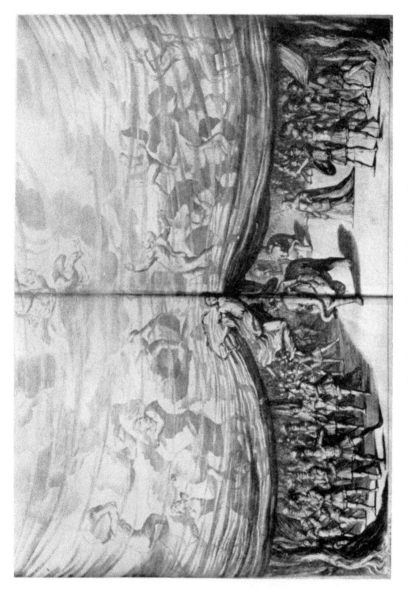

'*La Monarchia Latina Trionfante.*' *Prologue*

## B. *The Jesuit Drama and the Opera at Vienna*

The researches of Alexander von Weilen[1] into the Jesuit drama and the more recent volume by Flemming[2] comprising three important reprints of dramas and an illuminating study of the "Ordensdrama", now make it possible to survey in a general way the connections between the opera and the Jesuit plays. It is still, however, a matter of some difficulty to decide the exact nature of the relation from the point of view of the "mise-en-scène" (or indeed from any other). Whether the complicated stage technique was used first by the Jesuits in their school theatres or by the Court producers is uncertain. Jesuit performances were certainly known in Vienna long before the Court operas began. What is styled a "Jesuitenkomödie"[3] was performed as early as 1555, while the first scenario (or "perioche") in the German language of 1611 is actually said to contain an epilogue in which the apostle Matthew addresses the House of Hapsburg.[4] For this reason von Weilen calls it the first of the "Ludi Caesarei", as the Jesuit plays were later named to distinguish them from the operas.[5] The early plays performed in the Jesuit schools of Vienna belong in all probability to the humanistic tradition. This is certainly true in the case of the Latin drama 'Acolastus' of 1560 by the Dutch humanist Gnaphaeus.[6] The first really remarkable increase in scenic effects on the Jesuit

[1] In addition to the work mentioned above v. Weilen wrote one of the sections of the *Gesch. der Stadt Wien*, published by the Altertumsverein zu Wien and edited by Anton Mayer (Wien, 1918). The section referred to is in vol. vi, pp. 332–456: "Das Theater 1529–1740."

[2] *Das Ordensdrama*, Dt. Lit. Reihe xiii, Barock, Leipzig, 1930. An important earlier work is Flemming's *Gesch. des Jesuitentheaters in den Landen deutscher Zunge*, Berlin, 1923.

[3] The title is 'Euripus'. See v. Weilen, *Gesch. des Wiener Theaterwesens*, Wien, 1899, p. 17.

[4] v. Weilen, *ibid.* p. 23.

[5] According to v. Weilen a considerable rôle is played by Libussa's invocations of the spirits and her prophecies; this may be of interest to students of Grillparzer.

[6] v. Weilen, *Gesch. des Wiener Theaterwesens*, p. 17.

stages, seems, however, to coincide with Giovanni Burnacini's first appearance in the city. It is, therefore, extremely likely that he influenced the Jesuits to a considerable extent. The substitution of painted side-scenes ("coulisses") as a means of effecting rapid changes of scene for the "telari"[1] (three-sided prisms covered with painted canvas and revolving on a perpendicular axle) was evidently his idea.[2] It is interesting to note that a similar innovation was introduced at the Petit Bourbon in Paris by Giacomo Torelli, and we are told that the invention is usually ascribed to Torelli's teacher, Aleotti, in Florence.[3] Again we see the dependence of the stage at Vienna on Italian models. The actual form of the stage used by the Jesuits was based upon a plan designed by the above-named Joseph Furttenbach and published in his *Architectura recreationis* of 1640. This he had made from the models of Aleotti.[4]

The main aim of the Jesuit play was, of course, to educate the young to Catholicism, but it did so by displaying the power, wealth and authority of the Order, and the Austrian Emperors who preceded Leopold were not slow to realize that the victory of the Jesuits meant the ultimate extension and increase of the power of the Austrian Monarch as Head of the Holy Roman Empire. It was Ferdinand I who had sought help from Rome at a time when the Reformation had made such progress in Vienna that there were thirty Protestants to one Catholic.[5] Ferdinand II gave the Jesuits complete control of the university,[6] and he certainly had political reasons for desiring the triumph of Catholicism, his armies having defeated the Bohemian rebels supported by Protestants in 1620 at Prague.[7]

[1] From *tela*, i.e. cloth.
[2] Biach-Schiffmann, *op. cit.* p. 14.
[3] Biach-Schiffmann, *ibid.* p. 12.
[4] v. Weilen, *Gesch. des Wiener Theaterwesens*, p. 25.
[5] v. Weilen, *ibid.* p. 16.
[6] v. Weilen, *ibid.* p. 26.
[7] v. Weilen, *ibid.* p. 24.

The Order was at the height of its triumph under Ferdinand III and Leopold I, and the development of the Jesuit play runs parallel with that of the Venetian opera.[1] There was an intimate connection between the Court and the Order, for at first the Emperor himself took part in the public processions instituted by the Jesuits, and he was often present in person at the performances arranged by the Order. In fact, the Jesuit theatre seems to have been as much at the disposal of the Austrian Court as was its own theatre,[2] and it existed at any rate partly for the glorification of Catholic Austria and of the Hapsburgs as the Heads of the Empire. The desire of the Jesuits was not only to proclaim the victory of the Counter-Reformation, but the fame of the Hapsburgs who symbolized that triumph.[3] No play illustrates this better than does the famous 'Pietas Victrix', written by Nicolaus von Avancini and performed at Vienna as early as 1659, which, if it does not mark the beginning of the "Ludi Caesarei", as we have seen above, is at least one of the most important examples of the genre.

In the matter of performances there is one striking difference between Vienna and other Jesuit centres such as Augsburg, Munich and Ingolstadt, which suggests that the Jesuits of the capital were conscious of the necessity of competing with the great operatic pageants. Whereas in the dramas of both Jacob Bidermann and Jacob Balde[4] the interest focuses upon the fate of the hero and his mental conflicts, Nicolaus von Avancini, a Tyrolese nobleman and the most talented writer belonging to the Society of Jesus, lays the emphasis on the great state scenes and magnificent processions rather than on dramatic conflict. But it is perhaps

[1] v. Weilen, *ibid.* p. 24; cf. Nagl and Zeidler, *op. cit.* vol. 1, p. 663.
[2] v. Weilen, *Gesch. des Wiener Theaterwesens*, p. 24.
[3] H. Cysarz, *Deutsche Barockdichtung*, Leipzig, 1924, p. 222.
[4] Bidermann's most important play, 'Cenodoxus oder Der Doktor von Paris', was given at the Münchener Gymnasium in 1609 and in 1617 at Ingolstadt (see Flemming, *Das Ordensdrama*, p. 24); Balde's tragedy, 'Jephtias', at the university of Ingolstadt in 1637 (Flemming, *ibid.* p. 26).

unfair to compare these dramatists in this way, since Avancini really belongs to a later period[1] than the others—in fact to the age in which lavish display was becoming more and more the order of the day. The plays of Avancini seem to resemble the libretti in being merely texts or scenari of festival performances. Avancini even adopts the same practice of including engravings in the printed drama,[2] and of giving a large number of stage directions as marginal notes in the 1659 edition of the play.[3]

Success did not depend on good declamation and clever acting on the part of the students but on a great many other factors, such as scenery, design, illumination, machinery and so on. And indeed the Jesuit plays of the Counter-Reformation period were scarcely inferior to the Italian operas in magnificence of production. Their technique was astounding. Their keen sense of colour, their use of decoration, their skill in the handling of machinery and lighting effects, in short their power to captivate the senses of the audience, ensured the Jesuit theatre its popularity. The display and vivid colours of their costumes were more important than historical accuracy.[4] They could stage with ease great battles and naval encounters[5] and represent both heaven and hell with the semblance of reality.[6]

Opera and Jesuit play were closely allied in another respect; both introduced the comic interlude, a feature which added considerably to their attraction—which is not to say that the above-mentioned 'Pietas Victrix' contained any

[1] The dates are given by Flemming as follows: Bidermann 1578–1639; Balde 1604–68; Avancini 1612–86; see Flemming, *Das Ordensdrama*, pp. 23, 26.
[2] Flemming speaks of nine such copper-plate engravings on p. 367 of *Das Ordensdrama*.
[3] Flemming's reprint follows the second volume of the tragedies published in 1675. He adds on p. 367 of his volume the list of stage directions from the older copy.
[4] v. Weilen, *Gesch. des Wiener Theaterwesens*, p. 28.
[5] v. Weilen, *ibid.* p. 24.
[6] v. Weilen, *ibid.* p. 67.

comic episodes. Without seeing a number of the "periochae", it would be impossible to say to what extent comic treatment of characters or of situation is really indicated. Alexander von Weilen tells us that the chief characters in the comic scenes were boasting soldiers, clumsy servants, deceitful merchants and that in some of the plays there is evidence of impromptu acting in burlesque peasant scenes.[1] He mentions in this connection comic interludes in the religious plays of a Jesuit poet, Johann Baptist Adolf, who was born at Liegnitz in 1657;[2] von Weilen also states that the interludes indicated in the "periochae" by the successors of Avancini were comic. We have, however, this information only on the testimony of von Weilen, who may well have been carried away at times by enthusiasm for his subject.

In concluding this chapter it may be said that the Jesuit plays and the operas derive from the Italian Baroque. It is the Baroque stage of Italy that supplies the varied painted scenes, the art of perspective, the "machines" and the other "wonderful notions" of which Evelyn wrote in 1645 during his visit to Venice. And as in the opera with its love of pomp and exaggeration so there was in the Jesuit drama a marked tendency to subordinate content to form. Allegorical pageantry, political and historical allusions were placed before the portrayal of human passion. This very insistence on "externals", which characterizes not only opera and drama but every aspect of seventeenth-century life, was bound to be detrimental to the development of literature, overstressing as it did the practical demands of the theatre, emphasizing stage-craft rather than dramatic values, and thus preparing the way for the ultimate divorce of the theatre from the drama.

We have now to trace the development of the popular theatre at Vienna and to see what happened to operas in the hands of the directors of touring companies and popular

---

[1] v. Weilen, "Das Theater 1529–1740", p. 358.
[2] v. Weilen, *ibid.* p. 360; cf. *Gesch. des Wiener Theaterwesens*, p. 36.

actor-authors. Though it is not possible to discover exactly how, when and where any Court opera was adapted for the popular stage, there is, as we shall see presently, some evidence to show that certain plays were not taken directly from the Italian but from operas in the German language, which were translated and adapted from the original Italian operas. The play 'Atis' will serve as an illustration of the process of change from an opera to a popular play, since there exists in addition to the Italian 'Creso' the above-mentioned Hamburg libretto, from which the 'Atis' is obviously directly derived. After examining the repertoires of the player companies in Vienna between 1680 and 1722 and of the Kärntnertor Theatre, where popular plays were produced, it will be necessary to say something of the development of opera at Hamburg, in so far as it has any bearing upon our play 'Atis'.

## CHAPTER IV

## The Opera at Vienna and the Popular Theatre

Besides the Jesuit theatres for the educated classes of the community and the Court theatres for the aristocracy,[1] there was no regular theatre of any description in Vienna before the year 1708, when the Kärntnertor Theatre was opened and put in charge of an Italian touring company.[2] But it was natural under the circumstances that the common people, despised as they were and cut off from the other ranks of society, should seek amusement for themselves. This they found on the market-places, where they were entertained for hours on end by rope-dancers, acrobats and mountebanks. A passage from Abraham a Sancta Clara, who, though not a native of Vienna, was the most popular preacher there in the latter half of the century, throws light on the relations between clowns and doctors on the improvised stages of the market-places and public squares of the city. At a fair, he tells us, doctors, quacks and mountebanks would appear accompanied by their roguish servants. Pictures of Galen and Hippocrates were hung up near a stage erected on trestles and healing herbs were exhibited. The Charlatan or Pickle Herring indulged in all sorts of acrobatic tricks to attract the people and he was joined at times by a courtesan. With her he performed a comic scene at which the people laughed heartily and when the comedy was over and the market-place crowded with spectators, the doctor himself would mount the stage and begin vaunting his drugs. Gradually the crowd dispersed only to return with the re-

---

[1] Karl Weiss, *Die Wiener Haupt- und Staatsaktionen*, Wien, 1854, p. 35; cf. Nagl and Zeidler, *op. cit.* vol. i, p. 660, and Fritz Homeyer, "Stranitzkys Drama vom 'Heiligen Nepomuck'", *Palästra*, Berlin, 1907, vol. lxii, p. 6.

[2] v. Weilen, *Gesch. des Wiener Theaterwesens*, p. 124.

appearance of the fool who was able to sell his ointments to the bystanders much more effectively than the master whom he despised.[1]

With its quack-doctor entertainers on the market-places Vienna was not different from any of the other large German or Italian cities, for the Viennese preacher's description at once suggests Thomas Coryat's account of similar scenes in Venice at the beginning of the century.[2] The mountebanks and Pulcinella were just as popular with the mob on the Piazza del Castello at Naples or on the Piazza Navona at Rome, but in Italy at any rate the comedians did enjoy the patronage of the Courts. One actor Cecchini reckons in the year 1622 that he has served the family of the Gonzaga for thirty-five years.[3] But the Austrian Court took no interest in any form of theatrical entertainment beyond the opera and the Jesuit drama. Thus the travelling companies were left entirely to themselves[4] and they were often none too cordially received by the city authorities.

The decay of drama, no matter what its outward magnificence, was inevitable when the touring players were forced to throw in their lot with the quack doctors and there was no other alternative for them at Vienna, for the civic authorities about the middle of the century forbade the comedians to play except during the markets.[5]

This deplorable state of affairs changed, however, to some extent when the players were allowed into the so-called "Ballhäuser". Ball games had been introduced from Spain by Ferdinand I,[6] that is before 1564, and in addition to the

[1] v. Weilen, *Gesch. des Wiener Theaterwesens*, p. 115.
[2] Th. Coryat, *Crudities*, Glasgow, James MacLehose & Sons, 1905 (original 1611), vol. I, p. 411.
[3] K. M. Lea, *Italian Popular Comedy*, Oxford, 1934, vol. I, p. 280.
[4] E. Devrient, *Geschichte der deutschen Schauspielkunst*, Leipzig, 1848, vol. I, p. 121.
[5] Karl Glossy, *Theatergeschichtliche Ausstellung der Stadt Wien*, Wien, 1892, p. 25.
[6] v. Weilen, *Gesch. des Wiener Theaterwesens*, p. 116; cf. Glossy, *op. cit.* p. 26.

Court's "Ballhaus" there were three others in the city which were in time used for theatrical performances, one near the Franziscanerplatz being reserved for Italian companies, the German travelling players having exclusive use of another in the Teinfaltstrasse.[1] According to one authority the Italian troupes were the first to obtain a licence to produce plays for the public, and this as late as the year 1692.[2] No doubt enterprising directors, whether German or Italian, obtained complete texts of the Court operas (for they were all printed at Vienna by the press of Matteo Cosmerovio and his heirs)[3] and altered them to suit the coarse taste of their audience at the "Ballhaus" and the requirements of their own improvised stages.

Very little is known either of the personnel of the companies or of their repertoire from 1684 to 1720, itineraries and lists of plays of the troupes during this period having been neglected in favour of the study of those of the earlier seventeenth century, when English influence was dominant. While lack of information makes it impossible to follow the groups of players from place to place and the task of identification is difficult, it must be remembered that the plays, being the property of the director of a troupe, were hardly ever printed and that each company jealously guarded its own collection of plays. Certain pieces did, of course, pass from one group to another, probably when individual actors deserted and joined a rival troupe. The actors led a very precarious existence since permission to perform in a certain town was often refused them and yet for a livelihood they were dependent on their acting. The consequence was that they were obliged to submit at every turn to the taste of their audiences.[4] The choice of models was, therefore,

[1] v. Weilen, *Gesch. des Wiener Theaterwesens*, p. 116; cf. Moriz Enzinger, *Die Entwicklung des Wiener Theaters vom 16. zum 19. Jahrh.* Part I, Berlin, 1918, p. 6.
[2] Weiss, *op. cit.* p. 46.  [3] Homeyer, *op. cit.* p. 6.
[4] Flemming, "Haupt- und Staatsaktion", *Real-Lexikon*, ed. by P. Merker and W. Stammler, 1925–26, vol. I, p. 471.

governed entirely by the wishes of a public that desired to participate to some extent, even if only at the theatre, in the life of the Court and the aristocracy from which they were so completely cut off in real life.[1] They wanted at any rate some share in the magnificence and splendour which they themselves could never enjoy and incidentally to have some chance of hearing and seeing the exaggerations of the Court ridiculed by the actors' imitation. This must have given them a certain feeling of "Schadenfreude", for they enjoyed a joke at the expense of their superiors and were able to congratulate themselves on the superior depth and value of their own sound common-sense attitude to life.

As all classes were in a sense dependent upon the Court as the centre and head of society, the plots of the popular plays had to present kings or princes and princesses of the Court, ambassadors and persons of the highest rank. Thus the "Haupt- und Staatsaktionen" became a kind of substitute for the opera of the Court and the Jesuit drama,[2] and the easiest way for the actor-authors to obtain suitable plays was to take the texts of the favourite operas and adapt them. Comic parts could always be altered to suit a particular audience.

Although the lack of material makes it difficult to follow the players from place to place and to study the development of plays that held the popular stage, there is, it seems to me, sufficient evidence to prove that Italian plays were often adapted by the directors of the travelling companies. The description of these "Haupt- und Staatsaktionen" given by Gottsched and others suggests that they had their origin in the Court operas. It will only be necessary here to mention one such account, that of Velten's plays given by the historian of literature, Carl Friedrich Flögel, in his *Geschichte des Grotesk-Komischen*:[3]

Political events, amazing exploits of famous and legendary heroes and kings, the most sanguinary atrocities side by side with

[1] Flemming, *Real-Lexikon*, p. 471.    [2] Flemming, *ibid.* p. 471.
[3] Published in 1788, quotation from the edition of 1863, re-edited by Ebeling, 3 vols., 1863–69, p. 167.

the rhetorical affectation of princes and princesses and the most impertinent jests of buffoons, transformations, dreams, visions, heaven and hell, all in the most fantastic combination with solemn-allegorical-didactic figures, interludes, ballets, choruses, arias, illuminations and fireworks, these were the ingredients of Velten's "Hauptaktion", in alliance with the most extensive improvisation.

Every detail is reminiscent of the Court opera with the exception of the improvisation which was in fact all that the popular plays added to the operas.

But the main source of evidence is a collection of MSS. in the National Library at Vienna. Though it is impossible in the case of codex No. 13175, a play entitled 'Der Wollüstige Crösus in Lidien', to name any definite opera from which this play derives, it resembles a Venetian libretto as closely as does the 'Atis' which we know to be based on Minato's opera 'Creso', and like 'Atis', too, it bears the name of Karl Ludwig Hoffmann, director of the Elenson-Haacke troupe. The same is true of No. 13312, 'Comoedia Bestehend in 12 Personen' (though here there is no indication of authorship or date)—indeed many scenes of this play suggest the "commedia dell' arte" and the cast contains Mescolinus and Zavagninus as the servants of the two main characters. Mescolino was the mask of Pietro di Re about 1625, one of the actors who took the part of the Zanni.[1] Another character is Auretta; both the name and rôle assigned to her in the play suggest the Auretta who played the Fantesca in the Italian comedies.[2] There can be little doubt about the origin of codex No. 13149, 'Das Labyrinth der Liebe oder Amor, ein Lehrmeister listiger Zuschläge', dated 1722 and bearing Hoffmann's name, for the title-page contains a note to the effect that it is a translation from the Italian.[3] But the internal evidence is even more convincing, the names of the characters being Italian, the stage directions suggesting the

---

[1] Lea, *op. cit.* vol. II, p. 490.
[2] Lea, *ibid.* vol. II, p. 504.
[3] "Aus dem Italienischen übersetzt von Mr H. J. D."

elaborate decorations of the Italian opera, and the plot conforming closely to the ideal of the Venetian librettists. As far as No. 13125, 'Die getreue Sclavin Doris', dated 1720, is concerned, we have only to consult Gottsched's list of operas in the *Nöthiger Vorrath* to find that in 1680 an opera was performed in Hamburg with the title 'Doris oder der königliche Sklave' which had been adapted from the Italian.[1] A popular play of this name appeared on Daniel Treu's repertoire and on Meissner's list about the year 1700 which we have already mentioned.[2] The play in the National Library at Vienna closely resembles the Hamburg opera.[3] The arias of the opera are retained in verse form, though many of them are stroked out or bracketed together and followed by the stage direction "Prosa", indicating the intention of the players to convert them into prose dialogue. All the concluding verses were evidently to be omitted, for the word "Finis" is inserted a few pages before the actual end of the play. Corresponding to codex No. 12851, 'Der welterschröckende Attila', there is a Hamburg opera of the year 1682[4] and in the preface of this we are told that the material is taken from the Italian. Although the Hamburg 'Attila'[5] and the popular play are obviously related and the characters with few exceptions identical in both, there are sufficient differences to warrant the assumption that the play was not taken directly from the opera of 1682, but was based upon a second and different adaptation of the original

[1] *Nöthiger Vorrath zur Gesch. der dt. dramat. Dichtkunst*, 1757, p. 244; cf. *Hamburger Opernsammlung*, No. 11.

[2] Carl Heine, *op. cit.* p. 12; cf. Trautmann, *Jahrb. f. Münchener Gesch.* 1887, p. 257.

[3] The libretto was written by Johann Philipp Förtsch and the music by Nikolaus Adam Strungk; cf. F. Zelle, "J. Theile und N. A. Strungk", *Beiträge zur Gesch. der ältesten dt. Oper*, Berlin, 1891, vol. II, p. 15.

[4] Librettist: Lucas von Bostel (from the Italian by Matteo Noris of the Venetian school); cf. Flemming, *Die Oper*, Dt. Lit. Reihe XIII, Barock, Leipzig, 1933, p. 21; Zelle, *op. cit.* p. 14; Meissner, *op. cit.* vol. XIX, p. 146, No. 18.

[5] Music by J. W. Franck. Meissner mentions as the source Corneille's 'Attila' of 1667.

Italian opera. According to Homeyer, codex No. 12851 was adapted from the Hamburg opera of the year 1702, 'Der siegreiche König der Gothen: Alaricus, als Überwinder des mächtigen Roms'.[1] This is extremely unlikely, 'Alaricus' suggesting a different theme altogether, and it is much more probable that the Hamburg opera of 1702 was adapted from Steffani's opera 'Alarico' written for the Court of Munich in 1687.[2] Codex No. 13476 has, like many of the "Haupt- und Staatsaktionen", a very long title which, in accordance with the usual custom, indicated not only the name of the hero but the subject of the play: 'Der besiegte Obsieger Adalbertus König in Wälschlandt oder die Würkungen des Betruchs bey gezwungener Liebe mit H.W. [Hanswurst], Den betrogenen Breutigam, verwihrten Auffstecher, übl belohnten alten Weiber Spotter, gezwungenen Ehmann, Allamodischen Ambasadeur, *sehenden Blinden und hörenden Tauben*'.[3] The central theme of this play is Boccaccio's motive of the husband who falls a victim to his wife's deception, she succeeding in persuading him that he is both blind and dumb. The relation of the popular play to Boccaccio's tale is evident in the second part of the title which describes Hanswurst as "seeing blind and hearing dumb". The date of the play is given as 1724 (and not, as Heine suggests, 1774). It is identical with, in fact it *is* the 'Adalbertus' that occurred in the repertoire of Antoni Stranitzky, doctor and actor-author at Vienna in the early eighteenth century, and as the creator of the Viennese Hanswurst the most popular figure in the city. Fourteen of his plays which are extant in MSS. in the National Library were published in 1908 and 1910 by Payer von Thurn and are now easily accessible.[4]

Stranitzky was not, as Nicolai says, a native of Silesia, but

[1] Music by J. Chr. Schieferdecker. Homeyer, *op. cit.* p. 82.
[2] Schiedermair, *op. cit.* p. 28.
[3] Heine, *op. cit.* p. 7. From the MS. I have corrected the title as given by Heine.
[4] *Wiener Haupt- und Staatsaktionen*, Wien, 1908–10. For 'Adalbertus' see vol. II, p. 185.

of Styria. Very little is known of his life except that he seems to have combined with some considerable degree of success the callings of dentist, wine-merchant and comedian.[1] It is hardly necessary to assume that as a dentist he was better educated than the average strolling player of his time, if we are to believe the testimony of a document in the Stadt-bibliothek at Vienna, entitled "Narrenkalender auf das Jahr 1712". After describing the habits of the quack-doctors during their journeys from place to place the writer of the "Narrenkalender" continues: "Der Scharlatän rennet zur Universität hin, lässt sich auf eine Wurm-Cur examiniren, und wird aus einem Singer ein Artzt, oder aber aus einem Narren gar ein Doctor."[2] Indeed, if we are to judge by Stranitzky's own book, *Lustige Reyss-Beschreibung aus Saltzburg in verschiedene Länder*, which is a typical quack-doctor tale, obviously based upon the author's personal experience, Stranitzky must have served for a considerable period as the apprentice of a charlatan, a post for which he was no doubt admirably fitted by reason of his gifts as a comedian. On his way from Augsburg, Stranitzky appeared in Munich in 1699[3] and again in 1702 at Augsburg, on each occasion with puppets. Then for some time nothing more is heard of him until he appears at Vienna in 1705 as a "Commoediant" with his wife Maria Monica.[4] Here he joined a company of strolling players who performed in a wooden booth on the New Market-Place facing the gallows and the pillory! In 1706 he became joint director of the troupe with two other players, Johann Hilverding and Heinrich Naffzer,[5] and on being ordered to quit by the city authorities owing to the danger of fire, the players moved into the "Ballhaus" in the

---

[1] v. Thurn, *op. cit.* vol. I, p. xxxii.

[2] Hans Trutter, *Euphorion*, 1914, vol. XXI, p. 833.

[3] v. Weilen, *Gesch. des Wiener Theaterwesens*, p. 122; cf. v. Thurn, *op. cit.* vol. I, p. xx.

[4] v. Weilen, *Gesch. des Wiener Theaterwesens*, p. 122; cf. Gustav Gugitz, *Der weiland Kasperl*, Wien-Prag, 1922, p. 256.

[5] v. Thurn, *op. cit.* vol. I, p. xxi.

Teinfaltstrasse.[1] It is said, too, that at one time Stranitzky had a puppet-theatre on the square known as the Freyung.[2] It was when passing through Salzburg on his journey from Augsburg that he seems to have hit upon the idea of adopting the guise of a Salzburg peasant and as such he wore a pointed green hat and a short beard.[3] It was evidently only in the impromptu plays[4] that he appeared thus, for in the "Haupt- und Staatsaktionen" he seems to have changed his costume to suit whatever rôle he played[5] and usually came on the stage with a red heart (occasionally it was green!) sewn on the breast of his coat,[6] a very fit person to ridicule the Court amours which we have discussed above in Chapter II. Caught in a compromising situation and asked if he has a heart, he replies "Ja! auf dem Brustfleck".[7] In the introduction to his edition of the "Lustige Reyss-Beschreibung", R. M. Werner gives a description of the Viennese Hanswurst which is so interesting as to be worth quoting in full:[8]

The expressive countenance is adorned by a thick, short, black beard and a slight moustache, but the small tuft of hair below the lower lip is missing, so as to leave perfectly free the most characteristic feature of the face—the lips from which flow one jest after another. The hair is brushed straight back off the forehead and gathered together on the top of the head into a tuft like a crown. The costume consists of wide trousers stretching down to the ankles, where they are drawn in tightly, embroidered and trimmed with piping at the side-seams and the hem and held up by braces; a leather belt fastened by a clasp—into which a wooden baton[9] is thrust on the left side like a sword; a leather

[1] v. Thurn, *ibid.* vol. I, p. xxii.
[2] P. Leibrecht, *Zeugnisse und Nachweise zur Gesch. des Puppenspiels*, Freiburg, 1919, p. 32.
[3] Gugitz, *op. cit.* p. 256.
[4] Published in a book entitled *Ollapatrida des durchgetriebenen Fuchsmundi*, 1711, ed. by R. M. Werner, Wiener Neudrucke, 10, Wien, 1886.
[5] Weiss, *op. cit.* p. 47.
[6] v. Thurn, *op. cit.* vol. I, p. 31, also in the plays themselves ed. by v. Thurn, pp. 331, 350.
[7] v. Thurn, *op. cit.* vol. I, p. viii.
[8] *Lustige Reyss-Beschreibung aus Saltzburg in verschiedene Länder von J. A. Stranitzky*, Wiener Neudrucke, 6, Wien, 1883.    [9] "Pritsche."

breast-piece whose sole adornment is a green patch, shaped like a heart, sewn across the front on the left side and bearing on either side the initials H. W.[1] A ruff appears above the shirt at the neck and wrists, and over the shirt and breast-piece Hans Wurst wears a tight jacket with close-fitting sleeves and open at the neck. His hat of green felt is of the familiar peaked shape, and slung over his shoulder is a pouch in the form of a fat sausage. His feet are clad in light moccasins.

From the above it would seem not unlikely that Stranitzky was familiar with the Italian masks. The Harlequin had odd-shaped patches sewn on his clothes, while the tuft of hair on the crown is reminiscent of the rabbit scut on his small black cap,[2] and the pouch and wooden sword were often carried both by Arlecchino and Pulcinella, while the latter seldom appeared without the peaked hat or cap.[3]

Some idea of the burlesque type of play that was popular in the city in Stranitzky's time may be gained from the account given by Lady Mary Montagu in a letter of 4th September 1716 to Pope. The comedy performed on the occasion of the visit of the English ambassador's wife to the Kärntnertor was 'Amphitryon'. She writes:

I thought the house very low and dark; but I confess, the comedy admirably recompensed that defect. It began with Jupiter's falling in love out of a peep-hole in the clouds, and ended with the birth of Hercules. But what was most pleasant, was the use Jupiter made of his metamorphosis; for you no sooner saw him under the figure of Amphitrion, but, instead of flying to Alcmene, with the raptures Mr Dryden puts into his mouth, he sends for Amphitrion's taylor, and cheats him of a laced coat, and his banker of a bag of money, a Jew of a diamond ring, and bespeaks a great supper in his name; and the greatest part of the comedy turns upon poor Amphitrion's being tormented by these people for their debts. Mercury uses Sosias in the same manner. But I could not easily pardon the liberty the poet has taken of larding his play with, not only indecent expressions, but such gross words, as I don't think our mob will suffer from a mounte-bank. The two Sosias very fairly let down their breeches in the

[1] It almost seems as if Hanswurst's device is intended to burlesque the Emperor's custom of displaying the royal cyphers.
[2] Lea, *op. cit.* vol. I, p. 86.   [3] Lea, *ibid.* vol. I, p. 95.

direct view of the boxes, which were full of people of the first rank, that seemed very well pleased with their entertainment and they assured me that this was a celebrated piece.[1]

It is not easy to say whether Stranitzky acted in this play or not, though it is very likely that he did. He certainly appeared in his own play, 'Adalbertus', where one of the characters, Ernestus by name, was disguised as the God Mercury and was really mistaken for a God by Hanswurst,[2] who ran away in terror from his snaky wand.

Though 'Amphitryon' was no doubt based upon the French comedy, the repertoire of the Kärntnertor must have included many Italian plays. At least six of Stranitzky's "Haupt- und Staatsaktionen" are little better than translations of Italian libretti. The originals of his 'Adalbertus', of his 'Atalanta' and of his 'Der Tempel Diana'[3] were Italian operas, all written by Minato whom we know already as the Court poet of Vienna under Leopold I.[4] Stranitzky's 'Gordianus der Grosse' is based upon the Italian opera 'Gordino' by Cupeda who, like Minato, was a member of the Venetian school. 'Cafene' is Cupeda's opera 'La Fede Pubblica', which was performed by order of Leopold I at the Austrian Court in 1690.[5] Even where it is impossible to discover the original of a play, the internal evidence is such as to prove that it has its origin in an Italian opera. All of these plays follow the scheme already described above in Chapter II. But it is not likely that Stranitzky took the plays

[1] *Letters and Works of Lady Mary Montagu*, edited by her great-grandson Lord Wharncliffe, 3 vols. London, 1837, vol. I, p. 284. This "celebrated piece" may well have been similar to the play 'Von Amphitryone' produced by Velten at Dresden in 1678. In his history of the German Theatre Prutz quotes on p. 248 Christian Weise's description of its comic characters as follows: "Gestalt ich mich besinne, wie des Plauti Amphitruo an einen fürnehmen Orte praesentiret ward, da war Sosia Pickelhering, und da Mercurius seine Gestalt annahm, so kam ein Pickelhering über den andern, welches die Aktion sehr lustig und admirable machte."
[2] v. Thurn, *op. cit.* vol. II, p. 195.
[3] v. Weilen, *Gesch. des Wiener Theaterwesens*, p. 132.
[4] v. Weilen, *ibid.* p. 132.
[5] Homeyer, *op. cit.* p. 25.

directly from the Italian libretti. For at least two of his plays, 'Cosroes' and 'Atalanta', the existence of a German translation from the Italian which actually served him as a model has been proved.[1] 'Cosroes, der grossmütige Überwinder seiner selbst' is taken practically word for word from an opera of the same name, that was performed on the occasion of the Michaelismesse at Leipzig in 1708.[2] The text of this opera is contained in a collection of opera texts in the library of the Dom Gymnasium at Merseburg.[3] Trutter proves the word-for-word correspondence of the two texts and examines in detail a couple of scenes from each, showing that the rudiments even of the comic scenes were to be found in the Leipzig opera and that these scenes only required to be expanded and adapted so as to introduce such local allusions and jests as would amuse an audience at Vienna. Stranitzky's 'Atalanta' was probably adapted either from the Hamburg opera 'Die vereinigten Mitbuhler oder die siegende Atalanta', of 1698 or the earlier Leipzig version of 1695 by Strungk. The Italian original of all three operas was Draghi's 'Atalanta' for which Ludovico Burnacini designed the stage and scenery,[4] though it in its turn may have been adapted from an 'Atalanta' by Johann Kaspar Kerll performed in 1667 at the Court in Munich.[5]

As the centre of a movement to create a national opera in Germany, Leipzig was far surpassed by Hamburg and although it is difficult to establish a direct relation between Stranitzky's repertoire and the Hamburg opera, it is not by any means improbable that the Viennese comedian knew some of the Hamburg texts.[6] It is certainly true to say that Italian opera texts were translated for Hamburg, for Leipzig

[1] Homeyer, *op. cit.* p. 12.
[2] Hans Trutter, "Neue Forschung über Stranitzky und seine Werke", *Euphorion*, 1922, vol. xxiv, p. 323; cf. Schiedermair, *op. cit.* p. 35.
[3] Trutter, *op. cit.* p. 323.
[4] Biach-Schiffmann, *op. cit.* p. 137.
[5] Schiedermair, *op. cit.* p. 28.
[6] Trutter, *op. cit.* p. 322.

and for the popular Hanswurst stage in Vienna, and the connection between the latter and the opera at Hamburg was probably closer than is commonly supposed. Alexander von Weilen includes in his history of the theatres in Vienna on p. 316 one of the theatre bills of the Elenson company announcing a play with the title 'Le Bon Vivant oder Der Leipziger Jahrmarkt' to be performed at the Kärntnertor Theatre. This play was a loose adaptation of an opera given at Hamburg in 1710, 'Le bon Vivant oder die Leipziger Messe', and from the title and the description of the scenery given in the bill, it would seem that the Viennese text closely followed the Hamburg version.[1]

[1] Trutter, *ibid.* p. 317; cf. Glossy, *op. cit.* pp. 28, 29. According to the bill, the original of which is preserved in the Stadtbibliothek at Vienna, the author of the play was Ferdinand Felix Ellensonn.

## CHAPTER V

## 'Der Stumme Prinz Atis'; its relation to the Hamburg Opera and the Popular Theatre in Vienna

An opera-house was opened at Hamburg in the year 1678,[1] though we hear of opera being performed in the city twenty years earlier than that. In the first eighteen years of its existence, no fewer than 112 different operas were performed in the Hamburg opera-house, and as the opera developed splendour of production assumed the same importance as it had done in Vienna. Karl Goedeke tells us that one opera boasted of eighty-four different changes of scene and all manner of complicated stage devices.[2] For sheer magnificence of staging another opera far exceeded all expectations, a temple of Solomon being erected which created a real sensation in the city.[3] The "Audience-Sahl des Königs" or "ein Königl. Saal mit einem Thron" was an indispensable feature of the stage effects and the words "Herrligkeit" and "Grosse Magnificence" are used by contemporary writers in describing the scenes.[4] Sensational effects were even more sought after than in Vienna; in one scene of an opera, entitled 'Nebuchadnezzar', the King of Babylon appeared bound in fetters amongst the wild beasts of the desert with eagles' feathers growing on his head and claws instead of fingers.[5] That decorative stage effects were regarded as the most important part of the operatic performance in Hamburg may be gleaned from a study of the theatre bills and the libretti, where it was customary to enumerate the chief

[1] Kretzschmar, *op. cit.* p. 141.
[2] Karl Goedeke, *Grundriss zur Gesch. der dt. Dichtung*, Dresden, 1887, vol. III, p. 332.
[3] Flemming, *Die Oper*, p. 46.
[4] Flemming, *ibid.* p. 47.          [5] Flemming, *ibid.* p. 47.

decorative attractions.[1] Enough has been said to show that the Hamburg opera, in respect of its decorative accessories, did not differ to any great extent from its predecessor and model, the Venetian opera, as it was known at Vienna and the other Courts of the south—which is not to say that the Hamburg writers did not attempt to establish an independent opera. Nor did Hamburg depend entirely on Italy for its subjects, many being taken from French libretti and others from Dutch translations of Spanish dramas, not to mention oratorios, while some were based upon themes of local historical interest.

The play 'Atis' did not derive directly from Minato's opera, nor even from the first official German translation by Johann Albrecht Rudolph which appeared at ·Vienna in 1678, that is, in the year of publication of the original Italian libretto,[2] but from a German "Singspiel" adapted from the Italian opera. The "Singspiel" entitled 'Der Hochmüthige, Bestürtzte und Wieder-Erhobene Croesus',[3] is written, like the original libretto, in verse and is preceded by a synopsis outlining both the historical background taken from Herodotus and the intrigue invented by Minato. The synopsis is based upon the Italian argument which contained the "fatti storici" and the "accidenti verissimi", for we must remember that the Italian libretto usually confined the plot to the preface. Under the title are the words in brackets: "nach d. Ital. [=nach dem Italienischen] v. Luc. v. Bostel" and above the title "Joh. Phil. Förtsch". The libretto must therefore have been written by Lucas von Bostel, a doctor of law, who is known to have been successively alderman and burgomaster of Hamburg and who died in 1716.[4] This opera

[1] Flemming, *ibid*, p. 47.
[2] Copies of both the Italian and German texts are preserved in the Musikalien-Sammlung of the National Library, Vienna.
[3] I obtained photostats of the printed libretto from the *Hamburger Opernsammlung*, vol. I, No. 26.
[4] F. Zelle, "Joh. Phil. Förtsch", *Beiträge zur Gesch. der ältesten dt. Oper*, Berlin, 1893, vol. III, p. 5.

was performed in 1684 at Hamburg,[1] the music having been written by the composer Förtsch,[2] evidently a man of parts for he had studied medicine at Jena, matriculating in 1671, and had then travelled through Germany, Holland and France. He took lessons in composition with Johann Philipp Krieger, the noted organist at Bayreuth, who later became "Kapellmeister" in Weissenfels, the centre of the so-called "Liedoper".[3] In 1678 Förtsch went to Hamburg where he was for some time the chief tenor in the "Ratskapelle" and an opera singer.[4] He practised in 1681 as a doctor at Schleswig, then at Husum and wrote the texts of some twelve operas between 1684 and 1690.[5] At least six of these have their origins in Italian operas[6] and his 'Doris oder der königliche Sklave', performed in 1680 and included in Gottsched's list of operas for that year,[7] is, as we have seen above, one with the popular play 'Die getreue Sclavin Doris', just as Lucas von Bostel's 'Attila' of 1682 was, if not the direct model of 'Der welterschröckende Attila', at any rate nearly related to it.[8]

The 'Atis' so closely resembles the Hamburg 'Croesus' that it must have been taken from Bostel's opera and not directly from the Italian 'Creso'. It was probably on the repertoire of some troupe of strolling players at Hamburg and may have been brought to Vienna by the Haacke-Hoffmann company. That this troupe had some connection with Hamburg has been proved in Chapter II; some indirect evidence exists, too, in support of the assumption that 'Atis' was known to the popular theatre in Vienna. Three plays that,

---

[1] Goedeke, *op. cit.* (vol. III, p. 333) mentions a revised edition of 1711.
[2] Kretzschmar, *op. cit.* p. 142.
[3] Flemming, *Die Oper*, p. 69.
[4] Zelle, *op. cit.* p. 3.
[5] Flemming, *Die Oper*, p. 78.
[6] Zelle, *op. cit.* pp. 4–9.
[7] Gottsched, *Nötiger Vorrat*, p. 244; cf. *Hamburger Opernsammlung*, vol. I, No. 11.
[8] Zelle, *op. cit.* p. 14; cf. Meissner, *op. cit.* vol. XIX, p. 146.

44

to judge from their titles,[1] must have had much in common with 'Atis' were produced by Wallerotty, director of a player-company, in Frankfurt am Main, one on the 10th April 1741, another on 18th September of the same year and the third on 3rd January of the following year. Immediately prior to these performances, at any rate between 1740 and 1741, Wallerotty was joined by a number of actors who belonged to a Viennese company under the management of Gottfried Prehauser, Stranitzky's successor as Hanswurst at the Kärntnertor Theatre and the first to act the part of Lessing's Just in Vienna.[2] These actors were Franz Anton Nuth, the Harlequin of Prehauser's troupe in 1725, his wife Maria Anna Nuth, the Colombina, and Johann Felix von Kurz, Junior, who in the year 1738 became the most popular comedian at Vienna, and was known as "Bernardon".[3] Bearing in mind the dates of the Frankfort performances, it is not unreasonable to suppose that Wallerotty obtained the play 'Atis' from the actors who had at one time belonged to the Kärntnertor Theatre.

Having thus established the origin of the 'Atis' in Bostel's opera, it will now be possible to proceed to an examination of its structural elements and to a comparison of the popular play with Minato's 'Creso' and with Bostel's 'Croesus', the purpose of this analysis being to study how the Venetian opera was modified under German conditions to suit popular taste.

[1] (a) 'Der stumme Redner oder die Unbeständigkeit des Glückes, dargestellt in dem erstaunungswürdigen Fall des reichen Crösi'; (b) 'Der unglückseelige Reichthum oder der stumm gebohrene Redner mit Hans Wurst, einem lächerlichen Dolmetscher'; (c) 'Niemand soll sich vor dem Tode glücklich schätzen, oder die Würkung der Kindlichen Liebe'. See Heine, op. cit. p. 89.

[2] Glossy, op. cit. p. 23.

[3] E. Castle, "Österreichische Literatur", Real-Lexikon, ed. by P. Merker and W. Stammler, Berlin, 1926–28, vol. II, pp. 605, 609.

## CHAPTER VI

*Analysis of the Structural Elements of 'Atis'; Comparison with the Italian original 'Creso' and with Bostel's 'Croesus'*

A comparison of Bostel's 'Croesus' with Minato's libretto reveals that Bostel simplified the Italian opera and made it more effective from a dramatic point of view. While each act in the Italian has twenty scenes, Bostel's libretto has nineteen, sixteen and fifteen for the respective acts. The popular play 'Atis' is Bostel's text shortened and written in prose instead of verse. It has the same comic scenes, though in a more abbreviated form, and retains the verses which mark the conclusion of scenes and acts in Bostel's opera; in the opera these were arias.

'Atis' is, like its original, Minato's Italian opera, a "Hauptaktion" in three acts. This term was applied to the play of the "Wanderbühne" in the seventeenth century to distinguish it from the farce or "Nachspiel" often staged at the end of a performance. The division into three acts is to be found not only in the plays attributed to Stranitzky, which we have already discussed, but also in the popular Faust puppet-plays and many of the later Jesuit dramas.[1] The subject of 'Atis' is taken from Herodotus who tells how Croesus, the famous King of Lydia, once asked Solon, the Athenian law-giver, what happiness was, expecting to be told that he himself was the happiest of men. But Solon, conscious of the instability of human life, replied: "Call no man happy till he is dead." Herodotus further relates that Croesus was defeated by the Persians, and that a soldier of

---

[1] Cf. 'Bocoldus rex Hircaniae. Das ist: Johann Bocold, der gecrönte und nachmahls auff die alte Gaiss gesetzte Schneider von Leyden...', Dillingen, 1721 in P. Bahlmann, "Das Drama der Jesuiten", *Euphorion*, 1895, vol. II, p. 286.

the victorious army, not recognizing the king, attacked him with intent to kill him, whereupon the king's dumb son, Atis, in his fear, suddenly broke into speech and cried out: "Do not kill Croesus." After this defeat of the Lydians their king was taken prisoner and condemned to be burned alive, and as he stood on the pyre, he groaned, regretting his treatment of the wise Solon and muttering: "Call no man happy till he is dead." On hearing these words Cyrus repented of his cruel purpose, and at the last moment the Lydian king was saved by a violent rain which quenched the flames.[1]

This account of events by Herodotus supplied the main spectacular scenes of the Italian opera, round which Minato has interwoven the story of love and intrigue so characteristic of the opera of his time. The dumb Atis loves a Median princess at the Lydian Court. On recovering his speech in battle he devises a plan for putting to the test the constancy of his beloved Elmira and the fidelity of his courtiers. In the disguise of a peasant he returns from the war and enters the service of the princess, saying that he has been instructed to do so by his master Atis. Orsanes, a prince who also loves Elmira, sees in the peasant the means necessary to help him to usurp the royal power and win her hand in marriage. He asks the peasant to murder Atis, dress in the latter's clothes, pretend that he is the prince and resign his claim to the throne in favour of Orsanes. Atis is delighted at the chance of playing a double rôle, both to the discomfiture of Orsanes who dare not reveal the truth, lest his own treachery be discovered and also to the bewilderment of Elmira, whom he woos openly in the guise of the dumb prince (being driven thereto by Orsanes), but in secret as the love-lorn peasant, until circumstances force his hand and he must disclose his identity.

In the 'Atis' no alteration is made in the content and characters of the play, except in so far as the number of the

---

[1] *The History of Herodotus*, trans. into English by George Rawlinson, London, 1880, Book I, Chaps. 85–6.

latter is reduced and the love intrigue simplified. In this respect Bostel's text is followed closely. In the Italian libretto the chief characters, with the exception of the two kings and Solon, form a circle of lovers who rejoice or lament to each other, according as their suit is favoured or rejected. Atis, the prince, loves Elmira who returns his passion, Clerida loves Orsanes who pursues Elmira without success, while Eliates, who is proclaimed governor when Croesus goes to war, pays homage to Asteria who in her turn is in love with Atis. Thus two princesses are placed in contrast with Elmira, namely, Asteria and Clerida, and the grouping and conduct of the love affairs follows the technique of the literary pastoral. In the 'Atis' the general scheme is retained, though the plot is simplified by the omission of the rôle of Asteria. The unfortunate lovers bewail their fate just as they do in the Italian opera, though monologue and dialogue are substituted for the aria and recitative of the musical drama. In the 'Atis' the intrigue was obviously simplified in order to bring out well-defined contrasts between the good and the bad characters; indeed an intensification of the contrast was usually aimed at with the idea of impressing it on the audience. For example, Atis, the magnanimous prince and Eliates, the honest regent, form a double contrast with Orsanes, the selfish and dishonest villain, and both are in the end rewarded alike for their fidelity to the crown and the constancy of their love. This explains, too, why in the 'Atis' the part of Amiclea, Elmira's mother, is omitted altogether. In the Italian libretto it is she who is the regent, favouring the suit of Orsanes. But here Eliates, the governor, who in the absence of the king strives hard to promote the welfare of the people, and does everything in his power to liberate the Lydian king from captivity, can be contrasted effectively with Orsanes, who, in a similar position, intrigues against the interests of the state. Thus, though the German author does not shun copying whole scenes if he finds them suitable, he adapts his model in such a way as to satisfy the requirements of his own audience and his own stage. Similarly, he omits entire scenes if they do not in any way advance the plot, for here there is no preface such as was usual in the Italian opera, with an explanation of events to serve as a guide through the maze of intrigue. In the 'Atis' rimed arias are changed into prose monologues and these are interspersed with dialogue, the latter being more suitable for dramatic purposes. Arias are only left in their original form where they are required for special emphasis at the end of scenes or acts. The verses, for instance, are retained in the 'Atis' in almost exactly the form in which they occur in Bostel's opera: in Solon's speech before he leaves the stage in the first scene, again in the monologue of Cyrus after the defeat of the Lydians (Act I, Scene 17), and in Orsanes' monologue, when the king is ready to leave for the field of battle and the traitor sees his golden opportunity approaching (Act I, Scene 12).

It is in the comic scenes that we should expect to find the greatest difference between the Italian opera and the 'Atis', for comic situations must always be taken from contemporary life and manners or at any rate adapted to them. In the Venetian operas greedy servants, cowardly braggarts, ugly old beldames and saucy page-boys were familiar personages —all of them usual figures in Italian comedy, especially in the Commedia erudita. They supply the comic relief in Minato's 'Creso' and similar figures meet us again in the 'Atis', in scenes which have been interspersed at intervals, in order to provide entertainment for an audience that wanted a maximum of amusement with a minimum of effort. These scenes are introduced episodically and do not form a secondary plot. The first indication of a comic situation is contained in Act I, Scene 5, where the dumb prince makes love to Elmira by means of signs and gestures, and near the end of the scene we read the following stage direction: "N.B. Arlequin seine Voppereyen". The Harlequin is here evidently the young page-boy Neryllus, a character in 'Atis', and Carl Heine is probably right in assuming that the prince's behaviour was at this point caricatured by the jester. But he undoubtedly exaggerates when he says that the servant, Elcius, imitates and ridicules every movement of his master and parodies the latter's love-making, by wooing Neryllus, the confidante of Elmira.[1] Certainly there is no evidence for the truth of the second part of this assertion in the play itself, for Elcius is not present at all in the scene referred to and does not come on the stage until the following scene, as is obvious from the stage direction: "Elcius zu den Vorigen." Besides, in the Italian original and in Bostel's opera Neryllus is the pert little page-boy (a figure which had often been used by Plautus) who has to interpret to the princess the gestures of his dumb master, Atis,[2] and the old serving-maid is not called Neryllus but Trigesta[3] both in the operas and in the popular play. The scene would undoubtedly have lent itself admirably to a burlesque treatment, for the prince, being unable to express his feelings in the ordinary way, is obliged to resort to emphatic gestures, when his beloved asks him if he will always remain constant in his affections. Bostel's version gives at this point as a stage direction: "Atis giebet Zeichen einer brünstigen Liebe", but there is no trace either in the Italian or the German opera of a grotesque treatment of the foregoing scene. The "Voppereyen" indicate simply the intrusion of buffoonery, that is, of the horse-play and extempore wit that was common on the popular stage everywhere throughout the seventeenth century. The actor here no doubt made use of the usual comic effects of the wandering players, many of which must have been contributed by the "commedia dell' arte"; indeed the buffoon had a certain stock-in-trade of tricks that dates from the remotest antiquity. The antics and comic actions of the comedian were indicated only in a

[1] Heine, op. cit. p. 86.
[2] Bostel includes him in the dramatis personae thus: "Nerillus, des Printzen Atis kleiner Page."
[3] "Trigesta: der Printzeßin Elmira alte Bedientin" (Bostel).

general way in the printed texts. Probably in the case of 'Atis' the target of the actor's wit was the exaggeration of the Court manners, and owing to the acting and the local allusions this scene must have been much more effective than it seems to us to-day. While in Scene 5 there is nothing but the stage direction to guide us as to the nature of the comic episode and we are left to draw our own conclusions from it, the next scene (No. 6) indicates that the acting was intended to bring out the contrast between the characters of low degree and those of high rank. Following on love-making between the prince and princess, Elcius asks Neryllus if he feels ready for a piece of roast ox and a drink of Rhine wine and the reply being in the affirmative, he concludes that Neryllus is a thousand times more sensible than his master, the prince. This scene corresponds to Scenes 6 and 7 in Bostel's opera, where fuller details of the action are given. Here, when Atis and Elmira leave the stage, Elcius seizes the page and forces him to say (at least to sing) that he wants food and drink, obviously because that is what Elcius himself craves. Then the page-boy escapes leaving Elcius alone to sing:

> Ha! bon garçon, der Berenheuter
> Weiß recht hauptsächlich meinen Sinn,
> Daß ich ein guter Schlucker bin,
> Und tausendmahl gescheiter,
> Als mein Herr Atis ist.
> Der Tropff ist von der Liebe so besessen,
> Daß er dafür das trincken und das essen
> Fast gantz und gar vergist.
> Man wird durch andrer Schaden klug,
> Drum bin ich sicher gnug
> Daß Liebe nie bey mir kan hausen,
> Ich halte gar zu viel vom schmausen.

There is no organic connection between this scene and the preceding one, indeed as far as the plot is concerned, it could be easily omitted, but it was evidently included in the Hamburg opera and in the popular play to permit a burlesque treatment of the love-theme by the introduction of the minor characters, whose crass materialism could be opposed to and contrasted with the affected idealism of their superiors.

The same kind of burlesque treatment is indicated in Scenes 9 and 10 of the popular play, corresponding to 10 and 11 of Bostel's opera. In the ninth scene Elcius ridicules the opening words of Elmira, who, detecting some dissatisfaction in her lover, assures him that the light of his eyes is to her the sunlight. Elcius for his part would not like to depend on so poor a light, especially on a dark night and if he happened to be drunk. The reason for the prince's discontent is jealousy of his rival, Orsanes, and fear of inconstancy on the part of Elmira. Orsanes, Clerida and Eliates then bewail their disappointments in love, and in Scene 10, which is a monologue, the servant makes fun of the lovers, likening their complaints to the screeching of night-owls.[1] He himself does not take life so seriously, and any love-sickness he may feel is easily cured by a good draught of Rhine wine. The monologue corresponds to the aria in Scene 2 of Bostel's opera, which is preceded by twenty-four verses. Whether these were spoken or sung is not indicated in the libretto, but they show that Elcius was dressed as a gay court gallant with whirling plumes and rapier in hand and that he preferred striking blows, shooting or breaking necks to any dealings with the annoying little God Cupid. The burlesque spirit of the whole is apparent, and the popular "author" simply abbreviated the

[1] This may seem to us to-day a most peculiar comparison, but the sound of the "night-owls" was familiar enough in Hamburg, where in the local dialect the night-watchmen were known as the "Uhlen", presumably because of the noise they made. There were altogether two hundred of them in the city formed into a corps, called the "Rätelwacht" from the "Rätel" which was carried in the hand and had to be well rattled before the watchman's cry was heard. From 1671, the year of the establishment of the corps, we are told that complaints about the noise in the streets at night were extremely frequent. See R. Nehlsen, *Hamburgische Gesch. nach Quellen und Urkunden*, Hamburg, 1896, vol. II, pp. 213, 214; cf. *Idioticon Hamburgense ausgefertigt von Michael Richey*, Hamburg, 1755, p. 207: "Rätel-Kerls heissen in Hamburg die Nachtwächter, wegen der Klapper, womit dieselben, wie anderswo mit dem Horn, ihr Zeichen geben."

twenty-four verses by taking the first two: "Hört, wie die Eulen Für lauter Liebe heulen" to form the first line of the servant's monologue and then adding the aria that followed in Bostel with the alteration of only a very few words. These comic scenes are all the more interesting because they do not occur in the Italian libretto. In this the servant first appears with Prince Atis in Act I, Scene 15 (which corresponds to Scene 13 of 'Atis') when the prince takes leave of Elmira before the battle. He is the boasting "Capitano", equipped with all his accoutrements of war, bragging of his early return from the field of battle with a fractured hand or a bandaged head, mayhap with one eye lacking and extolling the wounds received in the defence of the Fatherland and the glory of a soldier's death. This scene may have been treated in a burlesque manner, too, in the Italian opera, for it forms part of the farewell scene between the lovers, when Elmira is about to send Atis to war telling him of the honour and the glory that reside in danger: "Vanne co' i Numi, e Vincitor ritorna!" The counterpart of this scene is No. 22, the last one of the act in the Italian libretto and the only other comic scene of Act I. Elcius enters dressed as a Persian. At heart he loves his food and drink and has seized the first opportunity after the defeat of the Lydians to strip a corpse and adopt the disguise that will best ensure his safety. Thus it is vain to speak of Mars and have wine in one's hand. As the moment has come for deeds not words, the boaster is humiliated, and the disclosure of his cowardice probably made a very good scene to conclude the act.

But Bostel in adapting 'Creso' evidently aimed at creating in the closing scenes of the act an uninterrupted series of impressive spectacles that would form a striking contrast to the opening scene of the play, and thus demonstrate to the audience the first stage of Croesus' fall from power and the idea underlying the whole play: "Call no man happy till he is dead." His arrangement was adopted in the 'Atis'. At the beginning the audience had seen the Court of Croesus, the king on his throne, his treasures displayed, and all save Solon paying homage to him. At the end no fewer than five scenes (they form only four in Bostel's opera, 16 to 19) are devoted to the visual representation of the change that suddenly overtakes a once-powerful king. Scene 14 of 'Atis' (it is 16 in Bostel's text) shows the two camps, the Persian one in the foreground, that is, occupying the most prominent position and indicating the ultimate victory of the Persian king. His triumph is further emphasized in the next scene (it is 17 in Bostel's opera) by his confident call to arms, by the presentation of the battle and the ensuing flight of the Lydians. In Scene 16 (18 in Bostel) Croesus, once mighty, now unarmed and stripped of his royal robes, is seen fleeing and saved from death by his son, only to fall into the hands of a Persian captain. Scene 17 shows the Persian victor riding in on horseback heralded by drums and trumpets, crowned with a wreath of laurels and surrounded by his soldiers and the captive Lydians. These four scenes in 'Atis' lead up to the final one in which, to the sound of the Persian cries of victory, Croesus is led forward into the presence of the enemy, captive but refusing to humble himself before the victor. The last two scenes of 'Atis' form only one in Bostel. Probably the intention of the "author" in creating two different scenes was to render more striking the contrast between the victorious Persian and the fettered Lydian. Any addition in the shape of a comic scene, such as exists in the Italian opera, would have tended to weaken the cumulative spectacular effect of the closing scenes.

The second act deals with the return of Atis to the Court in the disguise of a peasant and with the plan of Orsanes to usurp the throne. The traitor begins negotiations with the prince, the "peasant" makes love to Elmira and the Lydians offer half their treasure to save the life of Croesus. All this is taken directly from Bostel who followed the Italian text fairly closely, reducing, however, the number of scenes considerably. Once more, as in the first act, the important scenes occur at the end both in Bostel's libretto and in 'Atis' and indeed also in the Italian play, and are a pictorial representation of the turn in the tide of the king's fortunes. In the last scene but one Croesus again appears in chains before Cyrus who is seated on the royal throne in his tent. The Persian king refuses the treasure offered by the Lydian ambassador as ransom, and his victory is symbolized a second time by means of the spectacular effect of fireworks. The stage direction of the popular play "Wird ein Feuerwerck praesentirt unter Trompeten und Paucken-Schall" corresponds to that given not only in Bostel's but in the Italian text. The letting off of fireworks on the stage was a feature of the tradition derived by Vienna from Venice.

The only parts that differ to any considerable extent from the Italian opera are again the comic scenes, that is Nos. 1, 3, 14 of Bostel's libretto and of the popular play. While the fourteenth is lacking altogether in the Italian original, Nos. 1 and 3 of Bostel's text are based upon the exquisite rustic scenes of the Italian opera. In the first one Bostel follows the original closely. The scene shows a few country cottages with a peasant and his wife, some children, and two peasants playing, one on a pipe ("Schalmei") and the other on bagpipes ("Sackpfeife"). The old people and the children sing in turn, the young people repeating each time the aria sung by the parents. The gist of the song is a warning couched in playful terms to the children, telling of the birds caught by the fowler, then of the hinds that fall into the hunter's snare and finally of the dangers of Amor. There is a curious Anacreontic strain about the poems and indeed one is tempted to explain most of the features of the Venetian opera in terms of a debt to classical literature. One of the poems of Bion, the Greek pastoral writer, whose manner most closely resembled Anacreon's, tells of a boy-fowler who tried to ensnare the boy Love and who was warned of his danger by an old herdsman.

This scene, even as it stands in Bostel's text, must have

seemed unsuitable for a popular audience, and that is probably the reason why it is replaced in the 'Atis' by an extempore scene with only the stage direction: "Bauer und Bäuerinn mit ihren Kindern machen sich lustig und extemporiren was sie wollen." A scene like this must have depended upon the acting and may have been much more effective, considering the audience, than we can imagine to-day. The main object in including it at all in the popular play was evidently that nothing might be left to the imagination. It was not sufficient to tell a seventeenth-century audience, which always delighted in anything in the nature of a peep-show, that Atis acquired his disguise from the peasants. The peasants themselves had to be shown in flesh and blood, and hence the scene could not be omitted. Many examples of the inclusion of a, to us, un-necessary scene merely on account of its stage effectiveness are to be found in other seventeenth-century plays. A further striking example is the appearance of the disguised Jew in the 'Jud von Venedig' (adapted from Shakespeare's play by the "Englische Komödianten"), where it would be really sufficient for the audience, if it had any imagination, to hear that the Jew was going to assume a disguise in order to attain his ends. The scene was introduced to make the disguise palpable to the audience, that is to say, to spare the spectator any exercise of thought in identifying the means adopted by the Jew for his purpose.

The third scene of the second act in the Italian libretto is one of the charming "Villanelle" which was referred to above as the popular Neapolitan form of the madrigal in the sixteenth century. It is here a part-song of rustic character, written in a simple, light and airy style. It is wanton and, to use Thomas Morley's excellent description written in 1597 of the music of the madrigal, "wavering like the wind". The theme is amorous and charmingly frivolous and the thought, if one can here speak of anything so serious, is couched in words of delicate emotional, even erotic suggestion. Elcio, the servant, is on the stage with three country girls. Tired and worn out by his journey he lies down to rest in the lush grass of the meadow. One of the girls begs him to listen to their rustic song and he, mindful of the ease of the sylvan solitude (after the noise of war!), finds it easy to accede to her request. The country girl then sings of the beautiful shepherdess asleep in the meadow with flowers resting in her bosom (reminiscent of Amarantus' "lapful of flowers" in Sanna-zarro's 'Arcadia'), her hair hanging loose and whipping her forehead, while the playful breeze fondles her beauty and kisses her with its light breath. After each period of song there is a refrain when the other country girls join in. Elcius seems to find the entertainment to his liking, for he sings with the others in the last refrain, dances to the songs and then stops suddenly, still guided by his canny instinct, and says know-ingly: "Of the country children dancing to the sylvan song and of the noise of arms I have enough in the listening!"

The "Villanella" must have been a definitely aristocratic type of music and the expression of the highly cultivated life of an Italian court. The "villanelle" are no buxom country lasses used to hardship and privation but gentle shepherdesses who frequent the haunts beneath the waving poplars or the shady laurels or even myrtles, or nymphs beside the limpid fountains or the springs of sacred water. There is no trace in their song of rustic jests or of coarseness of speech. All is elegance. There is no real sensuality but only sensuous enjoyment. The ditties are not such as real country lasses would sing to beguile the time, for they express the feeling of longing (not even a real feeling) for the naïveté of the country of those who are wholly unacquainted with simple life. "We breathe here not the invigorating air of the country-side but the over-refined atmosphere of a pastoral convention."

Bostel seems to have realized the unsuitability of such a scene for a popular Hamburg audience and hence in adapting it, he changes its character completely. He, very wisely from the point of view of his audience, introduces Elcius at the moment when Atis, at the end of Scene 2, enters the hut to

57

negotiate with the peasants about his disguise. Elcius now appears not as the Court gallant but "in possirlicher Kleidung" as the Persian who has accommodated himself to circumstances and, as in the original, he dances and sings with the peasant children. For this Bostel evidently combined the last scene of Act I in the Italian ("Elcio goffamente vestito alla Persiana") and the country girls' song from Scene 3 of Act II. After explaining to the children his disguise, Elcius listens to their song which is a very free rendering of the Italian, introducing a certain coarseness that is absent in the original; we could, however, more easily imagine country girls singing Bostel's song. Elcius still remains true to his part of the servant with the capacious appetite. Now, with the king captured and the prince's whereabouts unknown, he is afraid that he may die of hunger. The corresponding scene in 'Atis' is the third, but again only the stage direction is given: "Elcius zu den Bauern in possirlichen Kleidern. Hat mit den Bauern seinen Discours und geht mit ihnen ab." It is very likely that Elcius here caricatured Atis who appears in the next scene asking whether his peasant's clothes suit him.

The next comic scene is No. 14 (it is also 14 in Bostel's libretto). In both, Elcius appears in the Persian camp as a travelling pedlar crying his wares, and as the scene occurs in a much longer and more detailed form in Bostel's text, probably it is his invention. The position of the scene in Bostel's opera and in the 'Atis' is significant, following as it does upon the instructions given by Orsanes to the "peasant-prince", authorizing him to kill the prince in his sleep, to throw his body from the window into the sea, then to put on the prince's clothes and act as if he were the dumb Atis. After this Elcius enters dressed as a pedlar carrying his pack. He describes how, on leaving the Persian camp, he was forced to beg and how, on being refused permission to do so by the authorities, he pushed a pedlar into the river and stole his possessions. There can be little doubt that this scene had some connection with the preceding one and that the successful pedlar-thief was contrasted with the unsuccessful throne-snatcher, much to the disadvantage of the latter. The long monologue of Elcius in Bostel is full of local allusions to the importunate Hamburg authorities who made a habit of squeezing taxes even out of the beggars and only occasionally relented, if flattered by a title such as "Excellenz". Bostel chose a type of comedy suitable to the Hamburg audience, and that was evidently the comedy of the market-place with its peasants, its mountebanks and charlatans.

If Bostel first adapted Minato's 'Creso' it was probably he who changed the comic scenes. Certainly there is evidence enough to show that the 'Atis' followed his version which was already adapted to a popular audience. In its endeavour to be popular the opera at Hamburg towards the close of the seventeenth century aimed at introducing comic scenes with topical allusions and the treatment was frequently burlesque; in fact, it was the exaggeration of the comic element that led to the ultimate failure of the opera in this city, as in other towns. Bostel did not even shun low buffoonery if it suited his purpose. In the year 1682, for example, he wrote a libretto entitled 'Cara Mustapha, der glückliche Grossvezir', in which the language of the love-scenes, introduced in imitation of Quinault, was so coarse that the performance called forth a storm of protest from the clergy, who proclaimed the opera to be a work of darkness. The opposition was led by the friend of the Pietist Spener, Anton Reiser, who had received and accepted a call to the Jacobikirche in 1681.[1] Reiser directed his attack not so much against the opera as against any form of theatrical entertainment. The clergy had every reason to be alarmed at the increasing popularity of the opera. It seemed indeed as if the stage had begun to compete successfully with the pulpit. Not only

[1] Reiser's pamphlet was entitled "Theatromanie, oder die Werke der Finsternis in denen öffentlichen Schauspielen". See Kretzschmar, *op. cit.* p. 142; cf. Flemming, *Die Oper*, p. 13.

were most of the earlier operas of the years 1678 and 1679 on biblical themes,[1] such as the Creation, the story of Esther, the birth of Christ, the mother of the Macabees and the destruction of Jerusalem, but Hinrich Elmenhorst, the preacher of St Catharine's, is said to have written many of the libretti.[2] Flemming definitely ascribes to him the introduction of comic characters, after the manner of Pickle Herring, into 'Esther' and 'Die Makkabäische Mutter'.[3] Certainly Elmenhorst had the last word to say in defence of the new opera against those Pietist opponents who dreaded the effects of its "Sinnenrausch" upon the people.[4]

The third act of 'Atis' shows how Orsanes is outwitted by the protagonist and fails to win the crown and the hand of the princess. The last five scenes (Nos. 15–19) were again obviously intended to present a gradual crescendo of spectacular effect and in this respect they follow the corresponding scenes not only of Bostel's opera (Nos. 14 and 15) but of the Italian opera. Scene 15 of 'Atis' symbolizes the power of the Persian king who occupies a throne in the front of the stage and is surrounded and protected by his body-guard, while Croesus is being undressed in preparation for the stake. The fire is lighted but is soon quenched by a sudden rain. In Scene 16 the fire is relighted just as the members of the Lydian Court appear on the stage and draw back in horror at the sight that meets their eyes. Atis offers his life to save his father and is dragged away as a madman, no one believing that he is the king's son. Scene 17 shows Croesus meditating before death upon the words of his wise law-giver,

[1] J. Geffcken, "Die ältesten Hamburgischen Opern, zunächst in Beziehung auf die in ihnen behandelte heilige Geschichte", *Zeitschrift des Vereins für Hamburgische Gesch.* 1851, vol. III, fasc. I, p. 35.

[2] That Elmenhorst was the author is definitely stated by Geffcken on p. 6 of the above article, while Kretzschmar and Flemming only admit the probability of his authorship (see Kretzschmar, *op. cit.* p. 142 and Flemming, *Die Oper*, p. 78).

[3] Flemming, *ibid.* p. 78.

[4] In 1688 he published a pamphlet "Dramatologia". See Kretzschmar, *op. cit.* p. 142.

whereupon Solon himself enters and repeats his warning about the transitory nature of earthly happiness. Cyrus, realizing that Croesus' fate may one day overtake him, repents of his cruelty and commands that the Lydian be set at liberty. In Scene 18 armed Lydians rush on to the stage in a last effort to save their king, whilst in the final scene the reconciliation of the two kings is brought about and we take leave of Croesus seated in royal robes beside Cyrus on the same throne. These five scenes of 'Atis' do not differ in any essential way from the two scenes to which they correspond in the operas. The increase in the number of scenes in the popular play must have been due to the lack of machinery on the popular stage. In the opera it was an easy matter to represent the thunder and lightning, the storm with the subsequent quenching of the flames and the relighting of the fire all in one scene. What was lost in spectacular effect on the popular stage (and judging by the list of properties it must have been as primitive as might well be) was made good to some extent by the greater prominence given in the 'Atis' to the re-appearance of Solon.

The comic scenes of the last act (Scenes 5 and 10) of the popular play are, like the corresponding scenes in Bostel's opera, recognition scenes. There is no trace of anything similar to No. 5 in the Italian opera though the tenth in Bostel's text is modelled upon the fourteenth scene of the last act of 'Creso'. In Scene 5 of 'Atis' Elcius, still a pedlar, returns to the Court, and not being recognized on his first appearance by the governor Eliates, he relates how he has come back with Olisius. Olisius in the Italian opera and in Bostel's was a Lydian prince who acted as ambassador to the Persian king. Apart from this scene, his name occurs in 'Atis' only in the dramatis personae, and three times in the text of Act III, Scene 16, on sheet 22 of the MS., namely twice in the margin and once in the stage direction, but crossed out each time and replaced by the name Halimachus. Possibly Halimachus played this small part in addition to his

61

own, but such an arrangement must have presented certain difficulties in our scene, where Halimachus is present in his own rôle. Perhaps he had to be retained here for the purpose of making a little more out of the comic scene, in which Elcius had to be recognized by a number of different people. It is also possible, of course, that the play was written down hastily and that the inconsistency remained unnoticed, though the first explanation is more plausible. Elcius is here brought together with members of the Court, so that he may speak his mind to those who are not all they ought to be, and in so doing he represents the man in the street. A study of the more detailed scene in Bostel's libretto is illuminating. Elcius is here half quack-doctor, half pedlar and he carries medicines in his pack for everyone—for Orsanes a plaster such as is worn on the shins by many widowers, bachelors and gallants —obviously a hit at the traitor's perilous adventure of entering the room of Atis by night with intent to murder. Then Elcius asks all present to bear witness to the truth of his statements, whereupon no one replies and he concludes that silence gives consent. The scene abounds in local allusions and must have been much more amusing than it seems to us now. Evidently spectacles were popular in those days with the Hamburg officials which explains why the pedlar carries such a large number in his pack and enters crying, "Brill, Brill, Brill." Before distributing his cures he turns to the audience and says:

> Vorerst muß ich euch lehren,
> Die Brillen artig zu verkauffen,
> Dadurch kommt man bei Hofe bald zu Ehren.

The most potent physic in the doctor-pedlar's pack is reserved for the governor himself. It is a medicine suitable for administering to the peasant classes and highly efficacious in squeezing out their last drop of blood, the reference being to the tyrannical methods employed by soldiers, bailiffs, magistrates and clerks who confiscate the property of the insolvent peasants and in due time appropriate it themselves. Hence the reference to the "Elexir proprietatis". With this physic the servant bestows a further gift in the shape of an "Almanac" which appears daily and publishes the names of all the candidates for "sweating, cupping and bloodletting". To this is attached a little statement—Elcius calls it an "Ein mahl ein"—to show that the balance is still on the right side, by indicating that the citizens will no longer put up with the selfishness and rapacity of their superiors. The Hamburg authorities, whatever their sins may have been, evidently had to submit to a considerable amount of criticism.

It is of interest to note that Bostel's opera was written in the very year when two powerful Hamburg citizens, Cordt Jastram and Hieronymus Schnittger, brought an accusation on various counts, without, however, submitting proofs for their statements, against the Burgomaster of the city. They succeeded in having him removed from office and replaced by a man who was completely under their control. Sudden suspensions from office, evictions, imprisonment without trial and more especially confiscation of property seem to have been the order of the day under the two powerful men who ruled, as we are told, like the thirty tyrants of Athens.[1] The plaster that Elcius gives Orsanes for his shins had a deeper significance to the Hamburg audience than it is possible for us to realize in reading the play to-day.

The last comic scene in Bostel's opera is the tenth which corresponds to Trigesta's monologue at the end of Scene 9, combined with Scene 10 of 'Atis'. Both the monologue and the general scheme of the scene are taken from the Italian libretto. Trigesta is the hideous hag with the skinny arms, familiar to us as the "Lena" of the Latin comedy, the garrulous old nurse of the academic comedy of the Renaissance and the "Ruffiana" of the "commedia dell' arte"—unfitted both on grounds of morality and integrity to be the guardian of her young mistress. Seeing this pedlar who does not at first

[1] Nehlsen, *op. cit.* vol. II, p. 249.

63

recognize her, she sends him about his business, whereupon he calls her an old powder-flask—a singularly apt description —which is the signal for a wordy battle in which each hurls vituperative remarks at the other. She says that she cannot be old, since beauty still adorns her face, at which he immediately puts on his spectacles the better to examine her and lo! he finds the well-known Trigesta. She in her turn recognizes the fool and questions him about his strange attire. To this he replies that he has become a merchant, thus giving her the eagerly awaited opportunity to vent her spleen upon the lazy profiteers. They, in her opinion, are good for nothing but drinking beer and wine, smoking tobacco and writing billets-doux to their mistresses. They are not even able to pay their bills to the coachmen, innkeepers and tailors, who are forced on that account to keep special book-keepers to do the dunning. Trigesta is so like the "Ruffiana" of the impromptu stage that she even carries with her her open pouch, into which Elcius drops a cosmetic for rejuvenating old women. Then there follows a song in praise of this aid to beauty, of snuff which is very fashionable with the dandies and finally, in the third and last stanza, of horns for making cuckolds, of which Elcius sells a prodigious number of pairs. On hearing a noise the couple withdraw, but not before Trigesta has made a request to the effect that Elcius shall come again.

The comedy of such a scene could only be thoroughly appreciated by those who understood all the local allusions, and the acting both in Bostel's opera and in the popular play was no doubt done in such a way that the servants were contrasted with the two princesses who come on the stage immediately after the exit of the servants. The position of the comic scene suggests such a burlesque treatment. It is preceded by the scene in which Atis hands Elmira a letter, begging her to love the peasant, Ermin, as the prince, at which she tears it up in a rage and sends him away. Immediately after the disappearance of the servants Clerida and

Elmira enter, both confused by the strange behaviour of the peasant-prince. They have resolved never to love again and sing over and over again: "Nein, nun will ich nicht mehr lieben." This is followed by Clerida's aria:

Amor hat mit meinem Schmertzen
Sein so saur gesaltznes Schertzen
Nunmehr lang genug getrieben.

To which Elmira replies:

Amor schöpffet nur Vergnügen
Mit Betrug und falschen Lügen
Treue Hertzen zu betrüben.

It need not surprise us to find so much less detail in the comic scenes of the popular play 'Atis'; all that the actors required beforehand was some guide as to the type of the scene, for this could never be played in exactly the same form in any two places, since the local allusions would have to be adapted to fit each case. But these topical allusions combined with the histrionic art of the actors probably ensured the success of such scenes with the audiences for whom they were intended.

# CONCLUSION

'Atis', a typical example of the class of plays known as "Haupt- und Staatsaktionen", presents us, both as regards the plot and the treatment of its various parts, with an odd medley of motifs which may be satisfactorily explained only in terms of their debt to the Venetian opera. Judging by such examples as 'La Monarchia Latina Trionfante' and 'Il Pomo d' Oro', the opera at Vienna was intended mainly as a great gala performance in honour of the power of the Emperor and of Hymen. Spectacular pageantry symbolized the authority of the Sovereign and the unity of the Empire, while Hymen was the symbol of marriage as a social institution. One of the most important features of the opera was the love intrigue, the conventional treatment of which is more easily understood with reference to its origin in the earlier pastoral drama. Even the "mise-en-scène" is, as we have seen, dependent to some extent upon the pastoral performances of the Italian Courts. Not only the elaborate and fantastic scenery, but the love intrigues taken from the Florentine operas, introduce into the operas an atmosphere of unreality. The plots cannot in any way be said to be based on actual life in Austria at the end of the seventeenth century, for the characters appear to belong to a dream-land and are just as unreal and artificial as those of the pastoral plays. It seems almost as if the despotic rulers, for whom the operas were written and before whom they were performed, were bent upon preventing their subjects from knowing what was happening in real life. Even the usurper's plot, held by Minato to be an indispensable part of the opera libretto, reflects the political life of Italy during the late Renaissance and has, therefore, little or no connection with German life, except in so far as the Court in seventeenth-century Germany was the pivot round which all social life revolved. The opera was intended to serve a social purpose. It was not concerned so much with the portrayal of life and passion as with the awakening in the audience of a sense of ideal harmony, such as we associate with a golden age. This harmony was brought about by the combined skill of the architect, the artist, the musician and the poet. It might be described as non-dramatic or even anti-dramatic, in so far as it is a threat to the clash of opposing wills without which no drama is possible. The "Staatsszenen" (so called, I think, in virtue of their splendour of production rather than because they dealt with state affairs) are inseparable from the cultural and social background of absolutism.

What the popular stage borrowed from the opera was the stereotyped form with the conventional themes, but with the primitive equipment at its disposal it was unable to imitate the magnificent theatrical effects of the Italian Baroque theatre. In fact it seems as if the actor-author of our play, in giving his modest list of properties,[1] was poking fun at the elaborate decorations of the Burnacini. In constructing the popular plays out of the operas, the music had to be dropped as being beyond the possibilities of the "Wanderbühne", and with the music the lyrical expressiveness of the original operas disappeared altogether. Dramatic conflict was as conspicuously lacking in the plays as it had been in the operas. Nor could a substitute for it be found in the startling stage effects of the operas.

A further marked defect of the plays (and of the libretti) is the complete absence of psychological analysis. It is clear from the account in Chapter VI that the plot of 'Atis' advances as the result of certain surprising and sometimes harrowing situations. The disguise of Atis as a peasant, or his rush to the pyre to save his father's life are examples of the one, while Croesus in captivity will serve to illustrate the

[1] "Eine Gießkanne mit Wasser, Thron, ein Tabulettkrahm, Calefonium, 2 Angeln, Hobelspähne zum Feuerwerck, 2 Fackeln, Babier."

other. These unexpected events, bringing sudden changes to the lives of the characters and creating a definite impression of movement, were as much a feature of the operas as of the "Haupt- und Staatsaktionen", and they were certainly more important for the development of the plot than psychological analysis. It should be mentioned that swift changes of fortune are likewise a feature of the later "commedia dell' arte".[1] The quality that is common to all three versions of the Croesus subject is the absence of character motivation. There is neither the analysis of the motives of an action nor of the effect of events upon the characters. To take one example only to illustrate this point: Cyrus, on hearing Solon's wise words and contemplating the sad spectacle of the ill-fated Lydian king in chains, becomes a different man, in fact the direct antithesis of what he was, but the change is in no way psychologically explained. For characterization we have here substituted a tangible and visible exposition of the idea, i.e. the transitoriness of human existence, which forms the main theme of 'Atis', as of the operas from which it springs; the place of characterization is taken by the pictorial presentation of contrasted characters and actions, resulting often in inconsequence of motive and inconsistency of character. The actual characters themselves are to be regarded not as individuals but as types with certain characteristics appropriate to their different parts, whether they be scorned or scornful lovers, successful wooers or rejected deserters, faithful, fickle or jealous. Orsanes is always the jealous lover and calculating intriguer, just as Atis is never other than constant in his love and faithful in his duty, both to his father and to the state. Barthold Feind who wrote a theory of the opera based upon his own observations of the Hamburg "Singspiel" says that each character must have a definite attitude of mind: "Ein Philosophus, Grosmühtiger, Verliebter, Verzweifelnder, Rasender, Misstrauischer, Eyfersüchtiger, Zweifelmühtiger, etc., muss nach seiner Gemühts-

---

[1] Lea, *op. cit.* vol. I, p. 103.

Beschaffenheit seine Person praesentiren."[1] But again in this respect the opera is very similar to all the Italian comedies that were based upon a love intrigue,[2] and one is tempted to come to the conclusion that the later "commedia dell' arte" must have been modified under the influence of the opera or at any rate that there was some approximation of the "commedia" and the opera.

The over-emphasis of theatrical art in the staging of the operas was one of the main causes of the gradual decline of dramatic art, as it manifests itself in the "Haupt- und Staatsaktionen". The effect of the "mise-en-scène" upon the structure of 'Atis', as of its models, is everywhere apparent. The form is governed by the arrangement of contrasting scenes in series which illustrate the general theme. These are not causally connected and some are necessary only in so far as they combine with others to illustrate and emphasize by means of stage effects the central idea underlying the whole.

Carl Heine was right and at the same time wrong, right in saying that 'Atis' derives from an Italian opera, wrong when he bases his assumption of the Italian origin upon the existence of burlesque scenes in 'Atis', for, as the above analysis has shown, they are the only part of the play that can really be called German, which is not to say that they have no relation at all with Italian, or indeed with earlier German, comedy. As has been mentioned already, a German translation of the 'Creso' was made at the Emperor's command, but to it Bostel owes little or nothing. Any originality displayed in the re-arrangement of the existing scenes and the addition of others, calculated to make the comedy topical, must be ascribed solely to the Hamburg librettist. It was Bostel who made a highly conventional type of Court performance suitable for an audience that knew no Court, by bringing it into contact with the real life of the city for which he wrote, and by establishing a connection between the actors themselves and the public. His happy allusions to the life of

[1] Flemming, *Die Oper*, p. 39.          [2] Lea, *op. cit.* vol. I, p. 102.

Hamburg, his satire on the vices of the times, made his opera genuinely popular, and it was largely because of the successful handling of the comic episodes that the play 'Atis' was able to hold the stage as late as the year 1742, when we are told that Wallerotty specially emphasized the burlesque treatment of such scenes as were intended to serve as a foil to the main action.

But the Venetian operas were highly unsuitable for imitation, being too artificial to hold the popular stage for long. What W. W. Greg says of the pastoral applies equally to the genre that derived from it: "It relied upon the accidents rather than the essentials of life."[1] It was only through the comic interlude in 'Croesus' that it was possible to establish real contact with the people for whom this opera was written. Bostel and his contemporaries in Hamburg, Christian Postel and Barthold Feind, succeeded in creating a popular opera (as far as it was possible to succeed in the circumstances), because of their skilful introduction of interests that appealed to the man in the street. In this sense Postel's intermezzi were more than mere imitations of Venetian operas; they introduced figures directly taken from the life, Bergedorf servants and vegetable-women and the peasants of the Marches speaking their dialect,[2] and even if no masterpiece was produced, there were promising indications that a national comic opera might develop. That this did not happen is due partly to the coarseness of the topical, farcical elements as Postel handled them; in a lesser degree to the repeated attacks of the Pietists against what they called the dangerous "Sinnenrausch" of the opera, but most of all to the final triumph of the Italian operas, with all their spectacular devices, until the closing down of the Hamburg Opera-House in 1738. And when Gottsched objects to the opera on the ground that it is a "blosses Sinnenwerk",[3] his view coincides

[1] Greg, *op. cit.* p. 421.
[2] Kretzschmar, *op. cit.* p. 145; cf. Schiedermair, *op. cit.* p. 44.
[3] Gottsched, *Versuch einer kritischen Dichtkunst*, Leipzig, 1742, vol. ii, p. 760.

strangely with that of such Pietists as Anton Reiser or Johannes Winckler, the friends of Spener, who inveighed against the opera at Hamburg—a coincidence of opinion due to the fact that a new age was at hand.

Gottsched had little difficulty in banishing Hanswurst from the German stage, but if the popular plays that were the offspring of foreign operas were not so easily ousted in Vienna, it was because of the popularity of the comic actors. Thus regular drama did not triumph over the "Haupt- und Staatsaktion" with its improvised burlesque scenes until 1770. Nor was that the end of impromptu acting. Vienna boasts of a long line of actors from Stranitzky to Nestroy, each of whom had something of the old Hanswurst. Though the scenic splendour of Italian opera seems so incompatible with the coarse realism of the Hanswurst scenes, an organic synthesis of the two unequal elements did become possible,[1] but only at Vienna. Here it was the impromptu stage that took over the foreign scenic effects characteristic of the Baroque opera, and united them with the farcical elements of the national Hanswurst comedy. Somehow or other, they merged into each other to form the "Zauberstück", a genre that is typically Viennese. It is true that the vast majority of the new magic plays did not appear until after the first performance of 'The Magic Flute' in 1791, but something of the success of Mozart's opera itself depended upon the introduction of spectacular scenes similar to those of the earlier Court operas and upon their combination with comic scenes that derived from the burlesque episodes of the "Haupt- und Staatsaktionen".[2] Schikaneder was well acquainted with the taste of the theatre-going public at Vienna when he included in his libretto the scene in which Sarastro is led in on a triumphal car, drawn by six lions and followed by a train of priests and attendants, not to mention others which betray

[1] W. Brecht, "Wien als Literaturstadt", *Wien, sein Boden und seine Gesch.* Wien, 1924, p. 468.
[2] Schiedermair, *op. cit.* p. 165.

their origin in the earlier operas. But Schikaneder knew too, that the "Theater auf der Wieden", of which he became Director in 1789,[1] had to compete with the theatre in the Leopoldstadt (the Viennese called it the "Lachtheater") which had been opened in 1781 and where Johann Laroche, better known as Kasperl, made his audience roar with laughter. Hence the insertion in the libretto of 'The Magic Flute' of the Papageno scenes which may with certainty be attributed to Schikaneder himself.[2] Tamino, with his golden flute to guard him from harm, has a comic counterpart in Papageno who receives a chime of bells, and whilst the hero has to go through the ordeal of silence, the garrulous fowler has for a time to put up with a padlock on his mouth, as a punishment for boasting and lying. Pamina's despair at parting from Tamino and her attempted suicide has a delightful foil[3] in the scene where Papageno, the healthy child of nature, usually satisfied with his food, drink and sleep, laments because of his lover's pangs, prepares to hang himself upon a tree and is like Pamina prevented just in the nick of time by the three Genii. The librettist must here have had in mind the tradition of the popular stage in Vienna, and indeed Papageno's part was created for none other than Schikaneder[4] —a mediocre librettist but a most skilful and gifted actor.

The sources of the "Zauberstück" were on the one hand the Jesuit drama and the Court opera, on the other the burlesque episodes of the "Haupt- und Staatsaktionen",[5] and its success depended mainly upon the art of the actors. The investigation of this type of play, however, and its relation to the opera and the "Haupt- und Staatsaktion", will form the subject of another inquiry, since it hardly falls within the scope of the present volume.

[1] Enzinger, op. cit. Part I, p. 11.
[2] E. J. Dent, Mozart's Operas. A critical study, London, 1913, pp. 355–8.
[3] Cf. Enzinger, op. cit. Part I, p. 308.    [4] Schiedermair, op. cit. p. 165.
[5] Otto Rommel, "Die Maschinenkomödie", Barocktradition im österreichisch-bayrischen Volkstheater (Dt. Lit. Reihe XIII, Barock), Leipzig, 1935, vol. I, p. 7.

# LIST OF LIBRETTI AND "HAUPT- UND STAATSAKTIONEN"

Minato, Niccolo. 'Creso.' Drama per Musica. Wien, 1678.

Rudolph, Johann Albrecht. Deutsche Bearbeitung 'Cresus', Gesungene Vorstellung..., Wien, 1678.

'Der Stumme Prinz Atis.' Codex No. 13107, National-Bibliothek, Wien.

Bostel, Lucas von. 'Der Hochmüthige, Bestürtzte und Wieder-Erhobene Croesus.' Singspiel. Hamburg, 1684. *Hamburger Opernsammlung*, vol. 1, No. 26.

'Das Labyrinth der Liebe oder Amor, ein Lehrmeister listiger Zuschläge'...aus dem Italienischen übersetzt von Mr H. J. D. geschrieben von J. F. G. in Augsburg, 1722. Codex No. 13149, National-Bibliothek, Wien.

'Der welterschröckende Attila.' Codex No. 12851, National-Bibliothek, Wien.

Bostel, Lucas von. 'Attila.' Singspiel nach dem Italienischen von Matteo Noris. Hamburg, 1682. Musikalien-Sammlung, National-Bibliothek, Wien.

'Die getreue Sclavin Doris.' Codex No. 13125, National-Bibliothek, Wien.

Förtsch, Johann Philipp. 'Doris oder der königliche Sklave.' Hamburg, 1680. *Hamburger Opernsammlung*, vol. 1, No. 11. Also in the Musikalien-Sammlung, National-Bibliothek, Wien.

'Der Besiegte Obsieger Adalbertus'...Componiert A° 1724 von einem Comico. (Stranitzky.) Codex No. 13476, National-Bibliothek, Wien.

Mozart, Wolfgang A. 'Die Zauberflöte.' Eine grosse Oper in zwei Aufzügen von Schikaneder. Wien, 1791. (Reprint of the first edition by Otto Rommel in "Die Maschinenkomödie", *Barocktradition im österreichisch-bayrischen Volkstheater*, vol. 1. Dt. Lit. Reihe xiii, Barock.)

'Der Wollüstige Crösus in Lidien.' Codex No. 13175, National-Bibliothek, Wien.

'Comoedia Bestehend in 12 Personen.' Codex No. 13312, National-Bibliothek, Wien.

# BIBLIOGRAPHY

Bahlmann, P. "Das Drama der Jesuiten." *Euphorion*, vol. II, p. 286. 1895.
Biach-Schiffmann, Flora. *Giovanni und Ludovico Burnacini, Theater und Feste am Wiener Hof.* Wien-Berlin, 1931.
Brecht, W. "Wien als Literaturstadt." *Wien, sein Boden und seine Geschichte.* Wien, 1924.
Castle, Edward. *Deutsche-Österreichische Literatur Geschichte.* 3 vols. Wien-Leipzig, 1926–30.
—— "Österreichische Literatur." *Real-Lexikon,* ed. by P. Merker and W. Stammler. Berlin, 1926–28, vol. II.
Collison-Morley, Lacy. *Italy after the Renaissance.* London, 1930.
Coryat, Thomas. *Crudities.* Glasgow, James MacLehose & Sons, 1905.
Cysarz, Herbert. *Deutsche Barockdichtung.* Leipzig, 1924.
Dent, E. J. *Mozart's Operas. A critical study.* London, 1913.
Devrient, Eduard. *Geschichte der deutschen Schauspielkunst.* 4 vols. Leipzig, 1848–61.
Doni, G. B. *Della musica scenica.* Firenze, 1763.
Dürrwächter, A. "Aus der Frühzeit des Jesuitendramas (nach Dillinger Manuskripten)." *Jhb. des hist. Vereins,* vol. IX. Dillingen, 1896.
Enzinger, Moriz. *Die Entwicklung des Wiener Theaters vom 16. zum 19. Jahrhundert,* in 2 parts. Schriften der Gesellschaft für Theatergeschichte, vol. XXVIII. Berlin, 1918.
Evelyn, John. *The Diary and Correspondence,* ed. by Will Bray. London, 1827.
Flemming, Willi. *Das Schauspiel der Wanderbühne.* Dt. Lit. Reihe XIII, Barock. Leipzig, 1931.
—— *Die Geschichte des Jesuitentheaters in den Landen deutscher Zunge.* Berlin, 1923.
—— "Haupt- und Staatsaktion." *Real-Lexikon,* ed. by P. Merker and W. Stammler. Berlin, 1925–26, vol. I.
—— *Die Oper.* Dt. Lit. Reihe XIII, Barock. Leipzig, 1933.
—— *Das Ordensdrama.* Dt. Lit. Reihe XIII, Barock. Leipzig, 1930.
Flögel, Carl Friedrich. *Geschichte des Grotesk-Komischen,* re-edited by Ebeling. 3 vols. 1863–69.
Fürstenau, Moritz. *Zur Geschichte der Musik und des Theaters am Hof zu Dresden.* 2 vols. Dresden, 1861–62.
Furttenbach, Josef. *Architectura recreationis.* Augsburg, 1640.
Geffcken, J. "Die ältesten Hamburgischen Opern, zunächst in Beziehung auf die in ihnen behandelte heilige Geschichte." *Zeitschrift des Vereins für Hamburgische Geschichte,* vol III, fasc. 1, pp. 34–55. 1851.
—— "Der erste Streit über die Zulässigkeit des Schauspiels." *Zeitschrift des Vereins für Hamburgische Geschichte,* vol. III, fasc. 1, p. 3. 1851.

Glossy, Karl. *Theatergeschichtliche Ausstellung der Stadt Wien*. Wien, 1892.
Goedeke, Karl. *Grundriss zur Geschichte der deutschen Dichtung*, vol. III. Dresden, 1887.
Gottsched. *Nöthiger Vorrath zur Geschichte der dt. dram. Dichtkunst*. Leipzig, 1757.
—— *Versuch einer kritischen Dichtkunst*. Leipzig, 1742.
Greg, W. W. *Pastoral Poetry and Pastoral Drama*. London, 1905.
Gregor, Joseph. *Wiener szenische Kunst*, vol. I, "Die Theaterdekoration". Wien, 1924.
Gugitz, Gustav. *Der weiland Kasperl*. Wien-Prag, 1922.
Haas, R. *Die Wiener Oper*. Wien-Budapest, 1926.
Hampe, Th. *Die Entwicklung des Theaterwesens in Nürnberg von der 2. Hälfte des 15. Jahrhunderts bis 1806*. Nürnberg, 1900.
Heine, Carl. *Das Schauspiel der deutschen Wanderbühne vor Gottsched*. Halle, 1889.
Herodotus, *History* trans. by George Rawlinson. London, 1880.
Homeyer, Fritz. "Stranitzkys Drama vom 'Heiligen Nepomuck'". *Palästra*, vol. LXII. Berlin, 1907.
Kaulfuss-Diesch, C. H. *Die Inszenierung des deutschen Dramas an der Wende des 16. und 17. Jahrhunderts*. Probefahrten, ed. by Albert Köster, vol. VII. Leipzig, 1905.
—— "Untersuchung über das Drama der Jesuiten im 17. Jahrhundert." *Archiv für das Studium der neueren Sprachen und Literaturen*, ed. by Alois Brandl and Heinrich Morf, vol. LXVII. 1913.
Kralik, R. von. *Geschichte der Stadt Wien*. Wien, 1926.
Kretzschmar, Hermann. *Geschichte der Oper*. Leipzig, 1919.
Kutscher, Arthur. *Das Salzburger Barocktheater*. Wien-Leipzig-München, 1924.
Lach, R. "Wien als Musikstadt." *Wien, sein Boden und seine Geschichte*. Wien, 1924.
Landau, Marcus. "*Die italienische Literatur am österreichischen Hofe*. Wien, 1879.
Lea, K. M. *Italian Popular Comedy*. 2 vols. Oxford, 1934.
Leibrecht, Philipp. *Zeugnisse und Nachweise zur Geschichte des Puppenspiels*. Freiburg, 1919.
Leichentritt, Hugo. *Reinhard Keiser in seinen Opern*. Berlin, 1901.
Lier, H. A. "Johannes Velten." *Allgemeine Deutsche Biographie*, vol. XXXIX, pp. 577–82.
Lord, Louis E. *The Orpheus of Politian and the Aminta of Tasso*. Oxford, 1931.
Meissner, J. "Die englischen Komödianten in Österreich." *Jahrb. der Shakespeare Gesellschaft*, vol. XIX. Weimar, 1884.
Mentzel, Elisabeth. *Geschichte der Schauspielkunst in Frankfurt am Main von ihren ersten Anfängen bis zur Eröffnung des städtischen Komödienhauses*. Frankfurt am Main, 1882.
Montagu, Lady Mary. *Letters and works*, ed. by her great-grandson Lord Wharncliffe. 3 vols. London, 1837.
Motta, Fabricio Carini. *Trattato sopra la struttura de' teatri e scene*. Guastallo, 1676.

Nagl and Zeidler. *Österreichische Literaturgeschichte.* Wien, 1899, vol. I.

Nchlsen, R. *Hamburgische Geschichte nach Quellen und Urkunden.* Hamburg, 1896.

Niessen, Carl. *Das Bühnenbild. Ein kulturgeschichtlicher Atlas.* Bonn, 1924/27.

Parry, C. Hubert H. "The Music of the Seventeenth Century." *Oxford Hist. of Music,* vol. III. 1938.

Reden-Esbeck, Friedrich Johann von. *Caroline Neuber und ihre Zeitgenossen. Ein Beitrag zur deutschen Kultur- und Theatergeschichte.* Leipzig, 1881.

Rettenpacher, Simon. *Selecta Dramata diversis temporibus conscripta et in scena recitata.* Salisburgi, Jan. Bapt. Mayr. 1683.

Richey, Michael. *Idioticon Hamburgense.* Hamburg, 1755.

Rommel, Otto. *Die Maschinenkomödie (Barocktradition im österreichisch-bayrischen Volkstheater,* vol. I). Dt. Lit. Reihe XIII, Barock. Leipzig, 1935.

—— *Nestroy und die Wiener Volkskomik.* Preface of *Nestroys Sämtliche Werke, Hist.-krit. Ausgabe,* ed. by F. Bruckner and O. Rommel, 15 vols. Wien, 1924–30.

—— *Die Entwicklung des Alt-Wiener Volkstheaters bis zum Auftreten Nestroys. Nestroys Werke,* vol. XV.

Sabbattini, Nicola. *Anleitung, Dekorationen und Theatermaschinen herzustellen,* 1639, German and Italian texts ed. by Willi Flemming. Weimar, 1926.

Schiedermair, Ludwig. *Die deutsche Oper.* Leipzig, 1930.

Schneider, Max. "Vorwort zu R. Keisers 'Crösus'." *Denkmäler der Tonkunst,* ed. by H. Kretzschmar, vols. XXXVII–XXXVIII. Leipzig, 1912.

Schütze, J. F. *Hamburgische Theatergeschichte.* Hamburg, 1794.

Stranitzky, Joseph Antoni. *Lustige Reyss-Beschreibung aus Saltzburg in verschiedene Länder.* Wiener Neudrucke, 6. Wien, 1883.

—— *Ollapatrida des durchgetriebenen Fuchsmundi,* 1711, ed. by R. M. Werner, Wiener Neudrucke, 10. Wien, 1886.

Symonds, J. A. *Renaissance in Italy. Italian Literature.* 2 vols. London, 1881.

Teuber, Oscar. *Geschichte des Prager Theaters, Von den Anfängen des Schauspielwesens bis auf die neueste Zeit.* Prag, 1883–88.

Thurn, Payer von. *Wiener Haupt- und Staatsaktionen.* Schriften des literarischen Vereins in Wien, vol. X. Wien, 1908; vol. XIII. Wien, 1910.

Trautmann, Karl. "Italienische Schauspieler am bayrischen Hofe." *Jahrb. f. Münchener Gesch.* 1887.

Trutter, Hans. "Neue Forschung über Stranitzky und seine Werke." *Euphorion,* vol. XXIV. 1922.

—— Review of Payer v. Thurn's *Wiener Haupt- und Staatsaktionen. Euphorion,* vol. XXI. 1914.

Vehse, Eduard. *Geschichte des österreichischen Hofes.* Geschichte der deutschen Höfe seit der Reformation, Part IV. Hamburg, 1852.

Voigt, F. A. "Reinhard Keisers Opern." *Viertelj. für Musikwissenschaft,* vol. VI, 2. Leipzig, 1890.

Weilen, Alexander von. *Das Theater 1529–1740.* Geschichte der Stadt Wien, publ. by the Altertumsverein zu Wien, ed. by Anton Mayer, vol. VI. Wien, 1918.

Weilen, Alexander von. *Die Theater Wiens. Geschichte des Wiener Theaterwesens von den ältesten Zeiten bis zu den Anfängen der Hoftheater*, vol. I, ed. by the Gesellschaft für vervielfältigende Kunst. Wien, 1899.

——*Zur Wiener Theatergeschichte.* Schriften des österr. Vereins für Bibliothekswesen. Wien, 1901.

Weisbach, Werner. *Der Barock als Kunst der Gegenreformation.* 1921.

—— *Die Kunst des Barock.* Propyläen Verlag. Berlin, 1924.

Weiss, Karl. *Die Wiener Haupt- und Staatsaktionen.* Wien, 1854.

Welsford, Enid. *The Court Masque.* Cambridge, 1927.

Zelle, F. "J. Theile und N. A. Strungk." *Beiträge zur Geschichte der ältesten deutschen Oper*, vol. II. Berlin, 1891.

—— "Joh. Phil. Förtsch." *Beiträge zur Geschichte der ältesten deutschen Oper*, vol. III. Berlin, 1893.

# INDEX

*Acolastus*, 23
*Adalbertus*, 35, 39
Adolf, Johann Baptist, 27
*Alarico*, opera by Steffani, 35
*Alaricus*, opera by Schieferdecker, 35
Aleotti, 24
*Amfiparnasso*, 12
*Aminta*, 10
*Amphitruo*, comedy by Plautus, 39
*Amphitryon*, popular play, 38 f.
Anacreon, 55
*Arcadia*, 57
Argenti, Agostino, 10
  *Lo Sfortunato*, 10
*Arianna*, 9, 11
*Atalanta*, opera by Draghi, 40
*Atalanta*, opera by Kerll, 40
*Atalanta*, opera by Steffani, 40
*Atalanta*, opera by Strunk, 40
*Atalanta*, play by Stranitzky, 39 f.
*Athys*, play by Rettenpacher, 3
*Atis*, popular play, ix, xi, 3, 28, 33, 42 ff., 46–66, 68 ff.
*Attila*, opera by Bostel and Franck, 34, 44
*Attila*, opera by Noris, 34
*Attila*, play by Corneille, 34
*Attila*, *Der welterschröckende*, popular play, 34, 44
Avancini, Nicolaus von, 25 f.
  *Pietas Victrix*, 25 f.

Balde, Jacob, 25
  *Jephtias*, 25
Bardi, Giovanni, 8
Baur, Johann Wilhelm, 6
Beccari, Agostino, 10
  *Sacrifizio*, 10
Bidermann, Jacob, 25
  *Cenodoxus*, 25
Bion, 55
Boccaccio, 35
*Bocoldus rex Hircaniae*, 46
*Bon Vivant, Le, oder der Leipziger Jahrmarkt*, 41
Bostel, Lucas von, 34, 43–6, 48–64, 69 f.
  *Attila*, 34
  *Cara Mustapha*, 59
  *Croesus*, xii, 43–64

Brunelleschi, 14
Bruni, Caletti, cf. Cavalli
Burnacini, Giovanni, 6 f., 16 ff., 22, 24, 67
Burnacini, Ludovico, 6 f., 16, 18 ff., 22, 40
Burnacini, Marc Antonio, 17, 22

*Cafene*, 39
*Cara Mustapha*, 59
Cavalli (Caletti Bruni), 6, 15
Cecca, 14
Cecchini, 30
*Cenodoxus*, 25
Cesti, Marc Antonio, 6, 18
  *Il Pomo d' Oro*, 18 f., 21
Charles VI, Emperor (1711–40), 3
Claudia Felicitas of Hapsburg-Tyrol, 5, 19
Contarina, 22
Corneille, Pierre, 34
  *Attila*, 34
Corsi, Jacopo, 9
Coryat, Thomas, 30
Cosmerovio, Matteo, 31
*Cosroes*, 40
*Creso*, opera by Minato and Draghi, xi f., 4, 28, 33, 44–65, 69
*Cresus*, opera by Rudolph (translation from the Italian), 43
*Croesus, Der Hochmüthige, Bestürtzte und Wieder-Erhobene*, opera by Bostel and Förtsch, xii, 43–65
*Crösus, Der Wollüstige...in Lidien*, popular play, 33
*Cupeda*, 39
*Cafene*, 39
*Gordino*, 39

*Dafne*, 9 f.
*Diana, Der Tempel*, 39
Doni, G. B., 8 f.
Dorcheus, M., 1, 3
*Doris, Die getreue Sclavin*, popular play, 34, 44
*Doris oder der königliche Sklave*, opera by Förtsch and Strungk, 34, 44
Draghi, Antonio, 4, 21, 40
  *Atalanta*, 40

79

Draghi (*cont.*)
  *Creso*, xi f., 4, 28, 33, 44–65, 69
  *La Monarchia Latina Trionfante*, 21, 66
Dryden, John, 38

Elenson, Andreas, 2, 33, 41
Elenson, Julius Franz, 2
Elenson, Maria Margarete, 2
Eleonora of Mantua, second wife of
  Ferdinand II, 5
Eleonora of Mantua, third wife of
  Ferdinand III, 4, 6
Eleonora von Pfalz-Neuburg, third
  wife of Leopold I, 4
Ellensonn, Ferdinand Felix, 41
  *Le Bon Vivant oder Der Leipziger
  Jahrmarkt*, 41
Elmenhorst, Hinrich, 60
  *Esther*, 60
  *Die Makkabäische Mutter*, 60
*Esther*, 60
*Euridice*, 9
Euripus, 23
Evelyn, John, 15, 27

Faust, puppet-play, 46
Feind, Barthold, 68, 70
Ferdinand I, Emperor (1558–64), 24,
  30
Ferdinand II, Emperor (1619–37), 5,
  24
Ferdinand III, Emperor (1637–57),
  5 f., 17, 25
Ferdinand, Duke of Tyrol, 5
Ferdinand Charles, Archduke, 5
Flögel, Carl Friedrich, 32
Förtsch, Johann Philipp, 34, 43, 44
  *Croesus*, xii, 43–65
  *Doris oder der königliche Sklave*, 34, 44
Francis I, King of France (1515–47), 15
Franck, J. W., 34
  *Attila*, 34, 44
*Fuoco Eterno, Il, Custodito dalle Vestali*, 19
Furttenbach, Josef, 14 ff., 24

Galeazzo, Gian, Duke of Milan, 14
*Gara, La*, 17 f.
Geffels, Franz, 19
Gnaphaeus, 23
  *Acolastus*, 23
*Golden Apple*, cf. *Pomo d' Oro, Il*
Gonzaga, family of, 8, 30
Gonzaga, Francesco, Cardinal, 10
Gonzaga, Vincenzo, Duke of Mantua, 5
*Gordianus der Grosse*, play by Stranitzky,
  39

Gordino, opera by Cupeda, 39
Gottsched, J. C., xi, 2, 32, 34, 44, 70 f.
Grillparzer, 23
Guarini, 10
  *Il Pastor Fido*, 10

Haacke, Johann Caspar, 1 f., 33, 44
Henry IV, King of France (1589–
  1610), 9, 15
Herodotus, 43, 46 f.
Hilverding, Johann, 36
Hoffmann, Karl Ludwig, 1 f., 33, 44

Isabella of Aragon, wife of Gian
  Galeazzo, Duke of Milan, 14

Jastram, Cordt, 63
*Jephtias*, 25
Joseph I, Emperor (1705–11), 22
*Jud von Venedig*, 56
Julia, Sophie, 2 f.

Kerll, Johann Kaspar, 40
  *Atalanta*, 40
Krieger, Johann Philipp, 44
Kurz, Johann Felix von, 45
Küsel, Matthäus, 19

*Labyrinth, Das...der Liebe*, 33
Laroche, Johann, 72
Leonardo da Vinci, 14
Leopold I, Emperor (1658–1705), 4,
  19, 20, 22, 24 f., 39
Leopold V of Tyrol, 5
Lessing, 45
*Libussa*, 23
Louis XIV, King of France (1643–
  1715), 15
Luise, Princess of Saxony, 9

*Magic Flute, The*, 71 f.
*Makkabäische Mutter, Die*, 60
Mantua, Duke of, cf. William
Margaret Elizabeth of Spain, first
  wife of Leopold I, 19 f.
Maximilan I, Emperor (1493–1518),
  5
Maximilian II, Emperor (1564–76), 5
Mazarin, 15, 17
Medici, Anne de', wife of Archduke
  Ferdinand Charles, 5
Medici, Claudia de', wife of Archduke
  Leopold V of Tyrol, 5
Medici, Marie de', wife of Henry IV,
  King of France, 9, 15

Minato, Niccolo, Count, 4, 7, 21, 39, 43, 46f., 49, 59, 66
Creso, xif., 4, 28, 33, 44–65, 69
La Monarchia Latina Trionfante, 21, 66
Monarchia Latina Trionfante, La, 21, 66
Montagu, Lady Mary, 38f.
Monteverde, Claudio, 8, 10 ff., 21
Arianna, 9, 11
Orfeo, 8, 10 f.
Morley, Thomas, 56
Motta, Fabricio, 16
Mozart, Amadeus Wolfgang, 71
The Magic Flute, 71 f.

Naffzer, Heinrich, 36
Nebuchadnezzar, 42
Nepomuck, Der Heilige, 29
Nestroy, 71
Neuber, Caroline, 1
Nicolai, Friedrich, 35
Noris, Matteo, 34
Attila, 34
Nuth, Franz Anton, 45
Nuth, Maria Anna, 45

Opitz, Martin, 9
Dafne, 9
Orfeo, opera by Alessandro Striggio and Monteverde, 8, 10f.
Orfeo, pastoral play by Politian, 10

Paradiso, Il, 14
Pastor Fido, Il, 10
Peri, Giacomo, 9
Dafne, 9
Pietas Victrix, 25f.
Plautus, 39
Amphitruo, 39
Politian, 10
Orfeo, 10
Pomo d' Oro, Il, 18f., 21, 66
Pope, Alexander, 38
Postel, Christian, 70
Prehauser, Gottfried, 45

Quinault, Philippe, 59

Re, Pietro di, 33
Reiser, Anton, 59, 71
Rettenpacher, Simon, 3f.
Athys, 3
Rinuccini, Ottavio, 9f., 15
Arianna, 9

Dafne, 9 f.
Euridice, 9
Rudolph, Johann Albrecht, 43

Sabbattini, Nicola, 16
Sacrifizio, 10
Sancta Clara, Abraham a (Ulrich Megerle), 29
Sannazarro, 57
Arcadia, 57
Sbarra, Francesco, 18
Il Pomo d' Oro, 18f., 21
Schieferdecker, J. Chr., 35
Alaricus, 35
Schikaneder, Emanuel, 71f.
The Magic Flute, 71f.
Schnittger, Hieronymus, 63
Schütz, Heinrich, 9
Dafne, 9
Sfortunato, Lo, 10
Spener, Jakob, 59, 71
Steffani, 35
Alarico, 35
Atalanta, Die siegende, 40
Stranitzky, Antoni, 35–40, 45f., 71
Adalbertus, 39
Atalanta, 39
Cosroes, 40
Gordianus der Grosse, 39
Der Heilige Nepomuck, 29
Der Tempel Diana, 39
Stranitzky, Maria Monica, 36
Striggio, Alessandro, 11
Striggio, Alessandro, son of the former, 11
Orfeo, 11
Strungk, Nikolaus Adam, 34, 40
Doris oder der königliche Sklave, 34, 44

Tasso, 10
Aminta, 10
Torelli, Giacomo, 14f., 17, 24
Treu, Daniel, 34

Vecchi, Orazio, 12
Amfiparnasso, 12
Velten, 2f., 32f., 39

Wallerotty, 45, 70
Weise, Christian, 39
William, Duke of Mantua, 5
Winckler, Johannes, 71

Ziani, 6

For EU product safety concerns, contact us at Calle de José Abascal, 56–1°,
28003 Madrid, Spain or eugpsr@cambridge.org.

www.ingramcontent.com/pod-product-compliance
Ingram Content Group UK Ltd.
Pitfield, Milton Keynes, MK11 3LW, UK
UKHW012337130625
459647UK00009B/334